Dearest Lisa

Passing the

lots of love
Grace

23-8-2020

Hoax Cuisine

Hoax Cuisine

Faking it in the Kitchen

Maggie Groff

SIMON & SCHUSTER
AUSTRALIA

HOAX CUISINE
First published in Australia in 2001 by
Simon & Schuster (Australia) Pty Limited
20 Barcoo Street, East Roseville NSW 2069

A Viacom Company
Sydney New York London Toronto Tokyo Singapore

© Maggie Groff 2001

National Library of Australia
Cataloguing-in-Publication data:

Groff, Maggie.
Hoax cuisine.

Includes index.
ISBN 0 7318 1026 0.

1. Cookery. 2. Quick and easy cookery. 3. Wit and humor.
I. Title.

641.55

Cover and text design by Greendot Design
Cover illustration by Katie Jordan
Illustrations on pages 36 and 120 by Hannah Groff
All other illustrations by Maggie Groff
Set in 12/14 Adobe Garamond by Asset Typesetting Pty Ltd
Printed in Australia by Griffin Press

All reasonable attempts were made by the publisher to contact copyright holders.

10 9 8 7 6 5 4 3 2 1

By the same author

Mothers Behaving Badly

Acknowledgments

Thanks to:

Jane Bastianon, Stella Groff, Pam Groff, Kitty Groff, Bambi Hanson, Mardi Hudson, Stella Hopkins, Kay McGraw, Allison Morgan, Rosa Piper and Ruth Thompson for their wonderful assistance with stories and recipes.

Selwa Anthony, Jody Lee and Bridget Howard for their professional services and superb advice.

My husband, Jay, for his tireless encouragement and constructive suggestions.

And special thanks to my daughter, Hannah, for her invaluable assistance with the illustrations.

For my father
Captain Herbert Johnson

Author's Note

The stories in this book are true. In certain instances I've changed names to protect the innocent. In others I haven't, as the innocent are quite capable of protecting themselves.

A word of caution. Some tales contain poignant insights into the secret workings of a woman's mind which may offend sensitive readers.

I live in hope.

Contents

Introduction

I wrote this book for you.

And me.

And every other busy woman who, clutching a six-pack of supermarket lamingtons, has staggered into a work lunch or school cake sale only to be greeted by a banquet of homemade delicacies from earth mother kitchens. Trust me, there's many an office do I've spent imagining the unfortunate demise of workmates as, one after another, we are rushed to the emergency room with botulism poisoning courtesy of someone's crab and anchovy tartlets.

I come from a place more fraught with catering peril than you could possibly imagine. I married into a family of hunter-gatherers where men brave the wilderness for meat and the rivers for fish, and women grow fruit and vegetables to bottle and preserve for winter months. Life is lived by bountiful seasons, and recipes are as old and trusted as the hunters' hills. Little wonder the family threw a wobbly when number one son married me, a Woolworths home delivery girl.

Faced with this unsporting competition, a passion for food and the demands of a full-time job, I created the gentle art of Hoax Cuisine solely to enhance my domestic image. Not for a minute did I believe the way to a man's heart was through his stomach. Quite frankly I couldn't give a horse's pitoot about the male alimentary canal. Besides, I've found more interesting bits.

I started my Hoax Cuisine adventures in a modest way by soaking the stickers off imported preserves and replacing them with my own fancy labels. Soon I graduated to more elaborate chicanery that involved discreet food transfer from shop freezer to Maggie bakeware. Next came professional disguise of pre-cooked chickens, the purchase of ready-made salads as green and glorious as a botanical garden, and to complete the image, artful chitchat peppered with foody words like rocket, crème fraiche, and bruschetta.

Time passed and I removed the sign from our fridge that said 'Food, like men, heads straight for your thighs' and replaced it with the firm reminder 'I made it myself'. I was a woman with a mission, and aided by an obliging supermarket, heavenly fruit and vegetables, earthy nuts, aromatic herbs and freshly baked breads, I created an image of gourmet proficiency. Me and Sara and the grocer. We were like that.

My first book *Mothers Behaving Badly* contained a smattering of Hoax Cuisine recipes. After publication I was swamped with letters requesting more timesaving tips and tricks on how to cheat on the domestic front. It appeared there were thousands of exhausted women in Australia (well, fourteen anyway) trying to keep their end up in the kitchen.

My husband set about building a large brick letterbox to

accommodate the fan mail, while I frightened the nation and prepared my infamous Skullduggery Jam on 'Good Morning Australia' and the 'Gold Coast News'; a big mistake as for weeks afterwards local shoppers scrutinised my trolley at the checkout and I had to clean up the Groff image, do hairdresser-type things, and stop eating Rolos in public.

I also took to the airwaves with tales of badly behaved women, recounting the escapades of family and friends. It was great fun and spawned phone-ins, competitions and death threats, as well as the idea for this book — the world's first cookery book of Hoax Cuisine complete with tales of badly behaved women. Once again Australia would lead the way. I couldn't sleep for two days worrying they'd make us a republic before I received a New Year's honour.

So ladies, here's the rub. It's time to eliminate those niggling earth mother demons and recapture domestic brownie points. It's time to fake the bake and take the credit. It's also time for me to go. Delia and Clarissa will be here any minute to help me do the pickled onions.

Sure they will.

Maggie Groff
New South Wales

Chapter One

Secret Women's Business

From 20 to 40 a woman needs good looks
From 40 to 60 a woman needs good friends
From 60 to 80 a woman needs money.

It doesn't say anything there about potato peelers and bread ovens, now does it?

What is Hoax Cuisine?

In a nutshell, Hoax Cuisine is part cheating and part real cooking, then passing the whole thing off as your own work. In broad terms it's fabulous shortcut cookery for women who prepare real food for a real family *every* day. And in even broader terms it's gourmet catering for women who like to cook and enjoy good food, but don't have time to create meals from scratch; women who never know how many will be eating, who is on a diet, who turned vegetarian, who hasn't eaten since yesterday, and who can't eat at all due to an unfortunate affair of the heart. In other words, Hoax Cuisine is for you!

How Does Hoax Cuisine Work?

The essence of Hoax Cuisine is to eliminate tiresome preparation steps, and with the assistance of top quality prepared products, fresh produce, aroma and illusion, create wonderful mouth-watering food to not only give your cooking a five-star rating, but also allow time to ensure that *you* are still the most delicious dish at the dinner table.

Keeping Up Appearances

I'm sure we'd all love to spend our days preparing interesting recipes from the dusty cookbooks in our kitchens, but we don't have time. Whether we work or not modern women are run ragged by daily commitments our grandmothers never imagined.

Grandma cooked breakfast and lunch, prepared a lavish afternoon tea, then washed up and commenced the evening meal. She also, bless her soul, laid the breakfast table before going to bed. Nowadays, of course, we are so dog-tired we lay ourselves on the breakfast table and pass out.

It's so unfair there is still an unspoken demand on us to produce the same level of domestic brilliance as Grandma. You've only to glance in women's magazines to see this unreasonable expectation is alive and kicking. The solution is to embrace Hoax Cuisine and cheat in the kitchen at every available opportunity. The golden rule is not to let anyone, including family, know you're doing so. Perception is everything. Time is your enemy. Secrecy and cunning are your weapons.

Go for it!

Quality Assurance: Q.A.

Don't you love this Quality Assurance lark? Pops up everywhere, doesn't it? Actually, Q.A. in Hoax Cuisine is very important. If you use the best quality fresh produce and top of the range prepared products you'll succeed every time. That's the beauty of Hoax Cuisine. It's so simple.

The Tuckerbag

Like Australia, it's enormous! From Tassie to Darwin there are shops jam-packed with tantalising delicacies itching to be decanted into your own containers, and fabulous natural dressings and elegant sauces waiting to be rebottled under your own label. I've taken into account that many Australians can't pop into a David Jones food hall and tempered recipes accordingly. As long as you have access to a major supermarket you can prepare most recipes in this book.

Despite this magnificent booty many of us are still suspicious of prepared foods, probably because the flavour and quality of goods on offer a few years back were pretty pedestrian. No one would have contemplated they could rival home cooking, except perhaps those who have eaten at Rosemary Misslebrook's house where even the dog eats out. Well, times have changed. These days there's gold, frankincense and myrrh in them there shopping aisles. And men!

Dollars and Sense

Unless you're cooking vast amounts of a particular dish, as in commercial catering, it's a fallacy to believe making everything yourself is cheaper than purchasing ready-made products. Every pantry in Australia contains an obscure, expensive ingredient that was used once then banished to the back of a shelf to fester and die. For my own part I'm the proud owner of one kilo of dried Kaffir lime leaves.

Are You Being Served?

I never understand statements at the end of recipes that announce 'Serves four'. Four what? Four lumberjacks from Nova Scotia? Four anorexics at a Melbourne Cup lunch? Four children who polished off the Tim Tams an hour ago? Well, I'm not playing that game. You're smart enough to figure out your own food to eater ratios.

The French Connection

What's in a name? Quite a lot when it comes to Hoax Cuisine. As any marketing consultant will tell you, if the product has a catchy name you could sell a pregnant rabbit to an Australian farmer. I have, however, been restrained in naming recipes here, otherwise you wouldn't have a clue what's going on.

Australia seems to have borrowed the best of international cookery, but whatever the origin there's nothing like creative language and a bit of frog to zap things up a bit. Consequently I spend a great deal of time in my kitchen cassouleting the odd bit of poulet à la small town in the Southern Alps. Like heck I do.

As a general rule the simpler the dish the more complex the name should be, and vice-versa. It's rather like being handed a business card. If the card bears the lone word 'Director' you know the person is the complete works, but if it declares 'Assistant Vice-President in charge of South Pacific Sales and Distribution' you know you've been passed an empty sandwich. Should get a few irate calls out of that statement ...

The exception to this French impressionist rule is when naming meals for children. They won't touch anything, repeat, anything, that sounds as though it's been interfered with by a foreign person in the kitchen. Unlike Mummy, who would give her right arm to be interfered with by a foreign person in the kitchen.

Damage Control in Hoax Cuisine

What do you do when you've cheated and someone asks for the recipe? Don't panic. People only request recipes out of politeness.

They have little intention of cooking the dish themselves.
 You have several options:

- Smile and promise to give them the recipe in a minute …
  and don't.
- Wax lyrical about the part of the meal you actually did
  prepare.
- Announce you will photocopy the recipe for everyone …
  and forget.
- Laugh with a silvery tinkle and say, 'Oh Sally, I gave it to
  you last time I made it!'
- Fall over and play dead like John Cleese in Fawlty Towers
  (my personal preference).
- Launch into a juicy piece of gossip.

 I know, I know, I've no idea how to laugh with a silvery tinkle
either.

Destroying the Evidence

There's no point in passing off a store-bought item as your own if
the foil tray is visible in the kitchen bin. The first person to walk in
will want to throw away a used tissue and discover your secret. There
are hard and fast rules if you wish to be a professional Hoax Cuisiner:

1. Unpack the shopping alone. This is the only serious
   drawback to Hoax Cuisine.
2. Frozen food must be left in the store plastic bag and
   placed at the back of the freezer until required. You must
   then dispose of wrapping in the outside bin.
3. Deli and food hall produce such as marinated sundried
   tomatoes, dips and sauces must be transferred to your own
   containers immediately, and packaging disposed of in the
   outside bin.
4. Receipts should be destroyed or hidden. Exactly as you do
   for clothes!
5. Food from speciality shops, such as French patisseries or
   gourmet take-aways, should also be transferred to your
   own cake tins or oven dishes.

Tip: If you don't wear glasses but still can't read the ridiculously small preparation instructions on ready-made food packaging and bottles, purchase a pair of cheap magnifying specs from the nearest $2 shop. Trust me, it will open up a whole new world. And save a fortune in phone calls to wrong numbers.

Tools of the Trade

Apart from the usual wedding presents there are several other items you will require. I won't insult you by explaining what may go in the freezer, fridge, oven or microwave.

You will need an assortment of the following:

- lots of interesting bottles for decanting savoury sauces and dressings
- jars to transfer jam and preserves into
- fancy labels so you can put your own name on the bottles and jars
- large ceramic platters for the alfresco serving touch
- small attractive jugs for dessert sauces
- rustic baskets for bread
- interesting salad bowls and serving dishes
- china, glass, pottery or Pyrex storage containers in various sizes with well-fitting lids. I don't like plastic as I can't hear when guests are nicking things out of the fridge. Besides, you mustn't put plastic directly onto the table — there is a reason cookery shows don't present food this way!
- several sizes of quiche, flan, and pie dishes to accommodate your favourite ready-made foods
- baking and pizza trays
- a large loaf tin.

- A mortar and pestle. Of course you won't be using these,
  but it's a good ruse to keep them upended on the draining
  board so it appears you've just mashed a few exotic spices.

Easy so far, isn't it? Before we go on I have to report a minor
mishap on the domestic front. It involves a physical altercation
between a moving vehicle and the new brick letterbox my husband
built to accommodate fan mail. The letterbox is not well. I was in
a hurry reversing out of the drive this morning and ran over it
while singing 'Do Wa Diddy' at full volume. I know. It could
happen to anyone. Yet another unfinished building project on the
premises ...

Chapter Two

Public Relations

This food is truly delicious
It's quite as good as mine,
I can't believe I made it;
How did I find the time?

— MAGGIE GROFF, CELL BLOCK H

Firstly I'd better give you an update on the letterbox fiasco. Things turned nasty. Four times I pointed out there wasn't a scratch on the family sedan. Anyway, to cut a long story short I haven't spoken to my husband for three days. He hasn't noticed yet. I'll keep you posted about this, pun intended, but for the moment it's time to dwell on the public relations aspects of Hoax Cuisine.

The Worker's Connection

Hoax Cuisine is for women who need to enhance their domestic resumé, and let's face it, who doesn't? It goes without saying we work too hard whether we are in paid employment or not, and it's our propensity for having unreasonable expectations of ourselves which unites us, not fuzzy stuff about tenderness and giving birth to new life.

And why wouldn't we have unreasonable expectations? We've been backed into a corner by public portrayals of extraordinarily competent females. Good grief, I've just read a novel about a woman who is a trained doctor and lawyer (aren't we all?), who can perform two post-mortems a day, survive an assassination attempt, have meaningful sex with a top government employee, resuscitate a senior police officer, solve a murder, and then drive forty kilometres through the worst snowstorm in American history to her fabulous house that she designed, and find the ingredients and prepare porcini polenta for four impromptu dinner guests. As one does.

Well, don't despair. Successful Hoax Cuisine will take you a step closer to this elusive Superwoman status. It provides the edge to advance your position in society, see you elected head of the school canteen committee, treasurer of the office Christmas party, spokesperson on women's issues to the United Nations, encourage you to even perhaps, perform the odd autopsy before lunch …

Public Perception

Apart from prancing around the office wearing a blue striped caterer's apron and waving a wooden spoon there are several things you can do, which don't involve food and its presentation, to enhance your success with Hoax Cuisine. As with Santa Claus and diamonds, overall perception is everything. Here are some easy suggestions:

- When a workmate or neighbour offers to pick something up for you from the shops, ask them to buy a small bottle of Spanish capers.
- Always have a 2 kg bag of flour visible in your trolley if shopping after work. You can replace it while the trolley is queuing at the checkout.
- Each time someone mentions the timesaving benefits of stir-fry, announce you think it's passé and waffle on about how food preferences in this country are going

Mediterranean. And incidentally I should point out
that hands-on preparation and cooking time for a
stir-fry is four times that of preparing a roast,
tossing it in the oven and walking away. I know, I've
timed it.
- Wax lyrical at morning tea on the vagaries of deboning
ducks and how icing sets too quickly in the heat.
- An occasional bandaid and the old cut-while-cooking
story work well.

You may think this is tongue-in-cheek, but it's not. Remember,
small acorns grow into beautiful oak trees.

The Gourmet Kitchen

You can have fun here, regardless of the basic kitchen you're working with. The aim is to make the kitchen look as if it's a happening
place in the cooking department.

The term 'gourmet kitchen', much touted by real estate agents
to add $10,000 to a property price, has nothing to do with cook-
ing at all. It signifies an ultra modern area gleaming with stainless
steel, an overhead rustic ladder dripping with copper pots, foreign
appliances that no one has time to use, and arty-farty pictures on
the walls. It bears no resemblance at all to your current interior
design of half-dead violets on the windowsill, a bowl of ageing fruit
on the bench, junior Picasso on the fridge and an assortment of
smelly shoes by the door.

The good news is that you are trying to sell yourself, not the
kitchen, and there are many things you can do to create the impression of a serious cook. You'll find the older the kitchen, the more
adventurous you will be.
- Place an attractive cooking pot, such as cast iron or
Le Creuset, on the stovetop at all times. This makes it
look as if you have just cooked something wonderful, or
are about to.
- Purchase a large wooden chopping board that means
business and keep it on the kitchen bench in full view,

not on its side out of sight. I use an enormous camphor board, which invites plenty of comments. It smells good too.

- A Perspex recipe bookstand is a must. Make sure you display appropriately difficult recipes at all times, and remember to change the page occasionally. *Vogue* recipe books are best for this.
- Hang a well-stained blue and white striped caterer's apron in full view.
- Stand a corked bottle of red wine next to the stove. This is an excellent gourmet touch, and, ahem, very useful for cooking.
- Kitchen utensils, such as wooden spoons etc, should be highly visible next to the stove.
- Jars of bottled produce should be on display — the ones now bearing your own labels!
- A disfigured and slightly burnt oven glove must be hung next to the oven. A clean tartan job won't impress anybody.
- Pin a large glossy food-oriented calendar on the wall and mark in imaginary dinner guests for all the Saturday nights. No one needs to know you watch 'The Bill'.
- Stand a small basket next to the stovetop and fill it with interesting bottles of olive oil, vinegars and salad dressings (with your own labels, of course).
- Remove African violets from the windowsill, and replace with herbs. Basil, dill, parsley and chives should also grow in big pots outside the kitchen door.
- Wine racks always give a good impression, so make sure there's one in your kitchen.
- You will need to display some form of real coffee preparation, either a percolator, plunger or filter system. Hide that jar of instant!

And for the more adventurous:
- Nail a rustic piece of wood to the wall, and hang bunches of dried herbs on it. This always looks artistic and gives

the impression you have grown them yourself —
Hoax Gardening!
- If your kitchen superstructure has seen better
days, distract attention from flaking plaster
by stencilling wine goblets in a line around
the kitchen wall. They look best at shoulder height.
Be creative and tip one goblet sideways with a few
drops leaking out.

There are a few no-nos when trying to design a kitchen to create the appearance of a modern gourmet cook in residence. The following is a list of things people often think denote catering proficiency, but in fact do the opposite:
- Spice racks. Most good cooks use fresh herbs, and spices
are kept in the dark, in drawers or cupboards.
- Coffee mugs on a stand.
- Ceramic teddy bear cookie jars.
- Bread bins.
- Tea towels from tourist spots. White caterer's towels with a
red or blue stripe give a better effect.
- Plastic containers of pasta or cereal. Replace these with
your own 'bottled produce'.

Crime and Punishment

Many people, and I'm one of them, have enormous trouble accepting compliments. The situation is compounded with Hoax Cuisine as there's the small matter of discomfort associated with accepting praise for something that wasn't entirely your own work. Those of you with unpleasant personality disorders won't understand what I'm talking about, but the rest of the country will need a straightjacket to stop them from singing like the three tenors.

It's hard to describe reaction to unwarranted praise. It's almost a cross between mild trepidation and involuntary smugness. You know that self-conscious feeling when you stop traffic on a busy road to walk over the crossing and you experience immense power and control as you tippy-toe in front of throbbing engines and annoyed motorists? Well, it's nothing like that.

The best reaction to catering adulation for Hoax Cuisine is to:

1. Smile
2. Say thank you
3. Suffer personal hang-ups in silence.

After all, if cheating in the kitchen is the worst sin you can commit, you must be rather special.

Chapter Three

Cooked Chickens

One cannot think well, love well, sleep well, if one has not dined well.

— VIRGINIA WOOLF (AND WITH A NAME LIKE THAT SHE'D KNOW A THING OR TWO ABOUT POULTRY)

Firstly I should inform you chickens are used to test aircraft windscreens. Dead chickens are fired from launchers to simulate a live bird in flight hitting a screen. I know this because I just heard a news report concerning a dismissed test mechanic who had been using frozen chickens ...

Tips for Buying Cooked Chickens

- Do comparison shopping in your neighbourhood to ascertain which store has the best plump, non-greasy birds.
- If possible purchase poultry not treated with steroids or hormones.
- Grain-fed or corn-fed birds are best. They generally have a yellow tinge.
- Stores which have a high turnover, and cook several batches a day, are less likely to sell a dried-out chicken that has been sitting under lights for five hours.

- If you have to park illegally outside the cooked chicken shop on the way home from work, avoid parking tickets by leaving your windscreen wipers on 'fast-wipe'.

The Recipes

It's tempting, I know, to tear a juicy cooked chicken into pieces and pile them onto a plate, but this does nothing for image or appetite. Don't worry; with the help of Hoax Cuisine you can create an impressive range of meals from the humble cooked chook. The first thing you do when arriving home is, of course, get a drink and fix your lippy. Then you hide the chicken bag and transfer the bird to your own baking dish so it appears you've just taken it from the oven.

There are many variations on this first recipe, and I've chosen my friend Edwina Lacey's version as, not only is it easy and delicious, but Edwina is the subject of this chapter's story. I've decided, in the interests of diplomacy and my future health, to have a guest recipe from each of the badly behaved women in my stories. Things should go swimmingly until Chapter Seventeen when there will be a slight glitch over Mary's recipe, because Mary is a gibbon.

The world's greatest nuts come from Australia

Edwina Lacey's Rainforest Chicken with Macadamias and Grapes

Edwina's delightful recipe is a showcase for the native rainforest nuts known as macadamias. The sophisticated blend of poultry, sweet grapes, crisp celery, and crunchy roasted nuts is perfect for a work lunch, picnic, or to impress overseas visitors. You can easily juggle quantities to accommodate needs.

You will need:

1 cup shelled macadamia nuts
(available from most supermarkets and health food stores)
1 cooked chicken
2 cups seedless green grapes
4 celery stalks, chopped
1½ cups good quality mayonnaise
1½ teaspoons curry powder
1 tablespoon soy sauce

Method: Roast macadamias in a moderate oven until lightly browned. Cut chicken into bite-sized pieces, discarding skin and bones (known in our house as 'invertebrating' a chicken). In a bowl combine chicken, grapes, celery and roasted macadamia nuts, keeping some aside. Mix together mayonnaise, curry power and soy sauce and stir through chicken mixture.
Presentation: Chill well. Place on an attractive serving dish and garnish with the extra roasted macadamias.

Edwina's Story

I hope you liked Edwina's recipe — she's a great cook, and very adventurous with food. I once saw her complete a school project about moths by pinning a corn chip on cotton wool, placing it in a small box, and writing a label that said 'SPECIMEN WING OF GENUS TORTILLA'. It was brilliant. I *knew* it was a corn chip and couldn't tell.

Eddy and I go back sixty thousand cappuccinos, almost to the days when coffee was coffee. It's a tremendous friendship and, no matter how long it's been since we spoke, we pick up where we left off — not a difficult task considering Eddy knows everything there is to know about everything, and I know the rest.

We call our chats 'girl-swap'. Eddy hurls abuse at the Liberal party, and tells me about secret goings-on at the university where she is currently employed. In exchange I tell Eddy about the new washing powder I'm using and other important household issues. Personally I don't think Eddy is impressed by my domestic abilities, but she never lets on. She's very thoughtful.

Eddy's attractive too, with oodles of blonde curly hair. She wears fabulous clothes and drives a green sports car, which is profoundly sensible when you have two children and a dog because you can't possibly take them all out at the same time. Eddy is very smart about that sort of thing. The dog is a large white poodle, and when it's in the car with Eddy and the sun is behind them they look like twins. You didn't know that, did you, Eddy? Maybe you should get Pom Pom a scarf scarf.

In addition to her university work Eddy has published papers, written books, chaired council meetings, visited Third World countries on aid missions, completed private consultancy work for major corporations, and quite honestly, it's enough to make you want to expectorate. She also has a doctorate in political science, and so many letters after her name they go right off the envelope. When I send mail, just to annoy her, I simply mark the front 'Mrs Lacey'. I can be a real worm sometimes.

Now that you've had enough of the incredible incredibleness of Edwina Lacey, I'm happy to inform you things are about to take a downward trajectory by way of a small career hiccough that occurred sixteen years ago. It still makes me glow with pleasure thinking of it.

Eddy's husband was an entrepreneur who owned a ski lodge in the Snowy Mountains. It operated as budget accommodation for students, and when Eddy wasn't running universities she took bookings, via telephone, from her desk at home, and settled deposits, payments and receipts by mail. Students refuse to surrender good beer money for a bank cheque, and it wasn't uncommon for Eddy to receive cash in the post and return change accordingly. Totally illegal of course, but then so was invading Poland.

At the same time Eddy was expanding her professional horizons and applied for a position with ASIO — the Australian equivalent of the CIA. She yearned to phone friends and say 'I can't tell you where I am', and longed to hide microfilm in a gap in a brick wall, but most of all I think she wanted a fountain pen that did everything except write words.

No one, even Eddy, knew what the job entailed, but intrepid Edwina spent hours at her desk and produced a glowing resumé. Nervously she popped the application in a postbox. Then we raced round to a mutual friend's house, which conveniently backed onto the ASIO compound in the Sydney suburb of Kirribilli. We hung a sign out of the upstairs window that said 'SAY YES TO EDDY', and waved at old unmarked ambulances as they drove in and out of the yard on surveillance missions. Sorry, ASIO. I've blown your cover on the ambulance thing. You'll have to start using something less obvious, like old fire engines. And no, it wasn't us that put the 'Virgin Megastore' sign on the Catholic girls' school up the road, although I do wish I'd thought of it.

Waiting for the reply was horrendous. Real floor pacing stuff. We filled anxious days by visiting the film set of a movie in which Eddy had invested money. On the first day it took three hours to drive there because Eddy was practising espionage manoeuvres in traffic trying to lose a number 26 bus, and we got hopelessly lost on a housing estate.

ASIO's reply arrived by special delivery; probably one of those invisible missing postmen who say you weren't home when they tried to deliver a parcel. It was bad news. ASIO thanked Doctor Lacey for her submission. ASIO regretted no position suitable at this point in time. ASIO returned her resumé. ASIO also returned the $20 note Doctor Lacey had attached to her resumé. ASIO regretted it did not assist with her application. Love, ASIO.

$20 note?

Eddy was crestfallen. Totally humiliated. She had inadvertently put $20 change from a student's ski booking in the wrong envelope. Of all the envelopes in all the postal systems in all the world, Eddy had to put it into ASIO's. They probably still laugh about it at personnel meetings. I hope so.

And talking of envelopes, sometimes when I don't feel like annoying Eddy by writing 'Mrs Lacey' on her mail, I use black felt pen and in extra large letters write 'Mrs 002' on the front. Just in case she has forgotten.

Next day by return of post I receive an envelope addressed to 'Mrs Mildred Ram's Bottom the Bullshit Artist Formerly Known As Maggie Groff'.

I told you she knows everything.

Time for my recipes ...

Barbeque Chicken with Apples and Walnuts

This mouth-watering dish is a variation on the traditional Waldorf, and wonderful on a warm summer evening. A bit like me.

You will need:

1 cooked chicken (well, imagine it's barbequed)
3 or 4 crisp red apples
2 tablespoons lemon juice
6 stalks celery, sliced
1 cup chopped walnuts
About 1 cup good quality mayonnaise
Celery leaves and a few chopped walnuts for garnish

Method: Discard skin and bones, and cut chicken into bite-sized pieces. Core and slice apples, leaving skin on, and toss in lemon juice to avoid discolouration. Combine with chicken. Add sliced celery and chopped walnuts and mix well. Stir through mayonnaise to the consistency you desire.

Presentation: Spoon salad onto a platter and garnish with celery leaves and chopped walnuts.

Alfresco Chicken Pesto with Sundried Tomatoes

This easy creation is great for picnics, summer nights and work lunches.
   You will need:

1 cooked chicken
250–500g pasta
(large penne or rigatoni. You can easily vary the amount)
1 cup black olives (I use Kalamata olives from the supermarket deli. Don't use bottled, because they have a different taste. And don't remove the pips.)
½ cup drained marinaded sundried tomatoes (bottled or deli)
1 jar basil pesto (there are many good bottled brands)
A few sprigs of fresh basil so it appears you made the pesto yourself. Which remember, you did!
A chunk of parmesan cheese for grating

Method: Discard skin and bones, and cut chicken into bite-sized pieces. Cook pasta, rinse under cold water and drain well. Combine pasta, chicken, olives and sundried tomatoes in a bowl. Stir through pesto to taste — start with about ½ cup and go from there. Remember, if you've used more pasta, you'll need more pesto.
Presentation: Place in a large Italian-looking bowl and garnish with a few sprigs of fresh basil and grated or shaved parmesan cheese.
Note: Freshly grated parmesan is *so* much better than pre-packaged grated, especially if someone sees you grating it. Even better is shaved parmesan. Ignore toffs who drone on about pecorino cheese — it's simply not as good on this dish.

Paella with Almonds and Coriander

This is one of my favourite recipes as the entire meal is cooked and served from one pan. Traditionally a Spanish dish (I've been informed the word 'paella' means cooked and served in the same pan), I have moved paella to Australia, stopping via France for a little *je ne sais quoi*. Don't be put off by the lengthy ingredients. It's great.

You will need:

3 tablespoons olive oil
2 cloves garlic, finely chopped
6 spring onions, roughly chopped
1 cup basmati rice
1 cup frozen peas
1 x 500ml box chicken stock
500ml water
A pinch each dried rosemary and thyme
1 bay leaf
Saffron or yellow food colouring powder (use saffron if possible)
1 cooked chicken, cut into bite-sized pieces
with skin and bones removed
1 red pepper, roughly chopped into 1cm sized pieces
½ cup slivered almonds, toasted or grilled until golden brown
2 cups large cooked prawns, shells removed
½ cup chopped fresh coriander

Method: Heat oil in a large electric frying pan (or a special paella pan) and cook spring onions and garlic. Add rice and toss in oil. Add peas. Pour stock and water over rice, and add dried herbs, bay leaf and prepared saffron or a pinch of yellow food colouring powder. Simmer uncovered until rice is cooked (about 15 minutes), taking care not to let it dry out. Add chicken, red pepper, almonds, prawns and coriander, and gently toss everything together.
Presentation: Serve immediately. As this dish is visually spectacular, I put the cooking pan on the table. Once you realise how easy and delicious this is you may even invest in a paella dish!

Bastille Chicken Salad with Fruit

Here is a recipe for the diet conscious. This tangy dish is also great
for using leftover chicken, and makes a good entrée or light salad
for lunch. It's called Bastille Chicken because the French were
always lopping people's heads off, the fastest way known to man to
lose five kilos of unsightly fat.

You will need:

½ cooked chicken
2 crisp Granny Smith apples
2 tablespoons lemon juice
1 cup pineapple pieces
Cottage cheese
1 iceberg lettuce
Fresh parsley

Method: Remove skin and bones from chicken and cut into bite-
sized pieces. Core and dice apples, leaving skin on, and toss in
lemon juice to avoid discolouration. Mix together chicken, apples
and pineapple, and stir through enough cottage cheese to achieve
desired consistency (amount varies depending on size of apples
and chicken).

Presentation: Wash lettuce carefully, trim leaves into a bowl shape,
and place on a serving platter. Spoon mixture onto leaves and
garnish with fresh parsley. I often prepare this for lunch, served
with an Eskimo Special (a glass of iced water). Then I eat a large
bowl of ice cream.

Tortillas with Chicken and Tomato Salsa

Quick, easy, and satisfying, this spicy combination is tortilla-filled perfection on a busy weeknight. If you're really pushed cheat and buy a good quality salsa, but true Hoax Cuisine cooks buy the tortillas and cooked chicken, and make the salsa.

You will need:

1 cooked chicken, cut into bite-sized pieces with
skin and bones removed
lettuce, shredded
1 packet of soft tortillas (in the supermarket bread department)

For the salsa:

4 ripe tomatoes, finely chopped
¼ red onion, finely chopped
1–2 tablespoons fresh coriander, chopped
2 tablespoons sweet chilli sauce

Method: To prepare salsa mix together tomatoes, red onion, fresh coriander, and sweet chilli sauce.

Presentation: Either wrap tortillas in the kitchen or place ingredients on the table for do-it-yourself enthusiasts. To wrap, place tortilla flat, add some lettuce, spoon chicken and salsa into the centre, turn bottom up and fold in sides to secure filling.

Chicken Balti

Who has fond memories of spending two hours cooking an Indian curry? Well, it's time for you to meet 'balti', the rage of Great Britain and Europe. Given time, 'balti' will overtake 'salsa' as the catchy cooky word-du-jour.

Quite simply, balti is a quick and delicious Indian curry with a strong coriander flavour. Traditionally it's prepared in a pot called a (wait for it) 'balti', but as you won't have one you can use a saucepan or electric frying pan. Balti cooking sauces are available in jars or cans from the supermarket. If you wish, follow directions on the can and cook chicken in the sauce. I prefer this super-quick and utterly scrumptious method with a ready-cooked chook.

You will need:

1 cooked chicken
2 tablespoons vegetable oil
1 white onion, chopped
1 can balti cooking sauce
Fresh coriander

Method: Cut chicken into bite-sized pieces, discarding skin and bones. Heat oil and fry onion. Add balti sauce and bring to the boil. Add chicken, and a little water if you want a 'wetter' sauce (but not too much — it should be the consistency of a stir-fry). Cover pan, and simmer gently for five minutes or until meat is heated through.

Presentation: You have two options. Spoon Chicken Balti into individual bowls and garnish with lots of chopped fresh coriander, or leave in the cooking pan, garnish with lots of chopped fresh coriander and serve at the table. I expect the choice depends very much on the state of your cooking pan.

Balti is best served with Indian naan bread. Experts tear off a bit of bread, and use it to scoop the balti into their mouths. As I do the laundry in this house, amateurs are made to use forks.

Letterbox Update

I figured this issue has become important enough to warrant its own heading. Neighbourhood male archaeologists can now be seen standing around the letterbox ruins in groups, doubled over with laughter. I am no longer allowed to reverse out of the driveway. All men are bastards.

Chapter Four

Seafood

As a child I went on many fishing expeditions with my father, and on days when the blighters wouldn't bite, and failure wasn't an option, we made a secret detour to Mr Claythorpe's fish shop and bought two shiny fat ring-ins to take home to Mum. One day I marched into old Claythorpe's to collect our 'catch', and pointed towards a tray of beautiful trout in the window.

'Nah,' said Mr Claythorpe, 'Yer Mummy phoned and said could I sell you cod today.'

Fish and Tips

- Shop at busy, clean establishments. Fish shops should smell of sea and ice, not dead fish. Remember, fresh fish have no smell!
- Whole fish should be firm with glistening skin and clear full eyes.
- Fillets should be firm and springy to touch.
- Raw prawns should be moist and translucent. Don't buy prawns with black spots on or under the shell — they are old.
- Cooked prawns should be pink and firm with full eyes. Shrivelled eyes denote age.

- Hard shell clams and mussels are sold live, and must only be purchased if the shell is closed. If it's open, the critter is dead. Don't buy it.
- All fish cooks should have a large patch or pot of dill — it's simply the best herb for serving with grilled fish. A lemon tree wouldn't go astray either.

The Recipes

We'll start our seafood cooking with a delightfully simple and deliciously succulent Atlantic salmon recipe from the kitchen of Mrs Audrey Ravenscroft. If there's a shortcut for anything, Audrey will know it, which is why she was my first port of call for a guest seafood recipe. Actually, that's a load of cobblers. Audrey's idea of cooking fish is taking a water taxi to Doyles — I only asked her for a recipe out of politeness. I'm still reeling from the magnificence of her offering. It's fabulous!

Audrey Ravenscroft's Poached Atlantic Salmon with Herb Mayonnaise

You will need:

Water
Juice of 1 lemon
Atlantic Salmon steaks or cutlets
1 bottle good quality herb mayonnaise (there are several on the market with different herb combinations — be original!)
Fresh dill to garnish

Method: Place enough water to cover steaks in a large frying pan. Add lemon juice and bring to the boil. Add salmon, reduce heat, and poach steaks for five to seven minutes until cooked. Meanwhile place a small amount of mayonnaise in a mixing bowl, and spread it around the sides so it appears you made it yourself.

Presentation: Drain salmon and place directly onto dinner plates. Spoon two to three tablespoons of herb mayonnaise over fish. Garnish with a sprig of dill placed artfully on the salmon. The remaining mayonnaise can be served at the table. It's a nice touch to let family and guests see you sampling the mayonnaise and nodding furiously. Reassurance that you've been busy!

Audrey's Story

I told you it was a fabulous recipe. Dear old Audrey's quite beside herself with culinary pride, and has even started putting parsley on the dog's dinner bowl.

I'm still having trouble imagining her standing up long enough to cook anything, as each time I see Audrey she is always prone on a sofa, on the chaise longue near the drinks cabinet, or in her pool reclining on a large pink floaty thing. Hard work never killed anyone, but I don't think Audrey wants to take chances.

Audrey is forty-five, but her use by date is two hundred and ten as not much has been used, and it's the devil of a job to describe her, as just when you've got a handle on her looks, she changes them. I suppose it's safe to say that Audrey has black curly hair, a short red bob, a blond chignon, and sixteen pairs of Christian Dior sunglasses. She also has the most exquisite hands and feet you've ever seen, not surprising when you learn she was a professional hand and foot model before retiring to take up lying down.

Aud's personality is tidal. One minute she bathes your soul with gentle loving waves, the next she's smashing you up against the pier in a force nine. Working out her tides is like weather forecasting — there's an eighty per cent failure rate. Many a time I've been desperate to relate an amusing incident, knowing Audrey will shriek with joy, only to find I'm having tea with Hannibal Lecter. This is, of course, why I like her so much.

Tommy, Audrey's husband, was an accountant. I say 'was' because he retired five years ago and took up annoying Audrey as a hobby because he couldn't play golf, and Aud refused to sleep with anyone who played bowls. Tommy's constant presence drove

Audrey round the bend, and we all took bets to see how long it would be before she got a part-time job. I had my money on volunteer work at the sleep research centre.

Audrey became very sullen and started going on long walks past the cemetery. I was very worried about her, and consequently became quite excited when I noticed an article in the local paper about the art gallery. They were asking, no, begging, for volunteers. I telephoned Audrey straight away.

Tommy answered. It was good to know he was still above ground. After a few pleasantries I asked to speak to Audrey.

'I'll try,' he said, and I heard him bellow out that I was on the phone.

'This is Audrey speaking,' said a curt voice. She left off the bit about coming round to rearrange my facial features if this wasn't important.

'The art gallery is looking for volunteers,' I said, getting straight to the point.

'I can't paint,' said Audrey.

'Audrey,' I said crossly, 'get off your high horse for a minute and listen.' I explained the art gallery was looking for guides and help in the gift shop. 'You'd be brilliant at it, Aud,' I said encouragingly, 'I can just see your beautiful hands pointing out a Matisse, or stroking a Degas ballerina.'

'I'm not lifting anything,' she said.

I was tempted to tell her that Tommy had once, in a drunken stupor, said he was going to bury Audrey standing up, but instead I gave her the phone number and made her write down the art gallery's address, just in case she had missed that huge building in the city. We talked a bit about Bosnia and a lot about Tommy driving her up the wall, and then Audrey had to go and lie down.

A few days later I saw Audrey at the hairdresser's. She looked radiant and was, as you guessed, lying back having her scalp massaged.

'How's the art gallery?' I asked, feeling sure this was the reason for her glowing disposition.

'Wouldn't have a clue,' she said gaily.

'Didn't you call them?' I asked crossly.

'Yes,' she replied, 'and thank you so much for putting me on to them.'

Audrey had to sit up while a girl called Raychill set about her head with a paintbrush and cooking foil.

'I went there,' said Audrey, patting my hand. 'I took tea with the head of the volunteers committee. Her name is Cynthia Braithwaite.'

'Yes,' I said, 'and …'

It was like getting blood out of a stone.

'She didn't like me,' said Audrey, and she sniffed loudly, momentarily disgusted by Cynthia Braithwaite's lack of good judgement.

'Oh, I'm sure she did, Aud,' I said, 'she would have loved you. Everyone does.' Raychill gave me an odd look. Obviously not a member of the Audrey Ravenscroft fan club.

'No, she didn't,' said Audrey, 'she hated me. I called her Snithia.'

'What!' I said, 'why did you call her that?'

'She looked like a Snithia. She had one of those sticky-up noses. And a little sticky-out tea finger.'

'Oh, Aud,' I sighed. She can be so exasperating.

'Anyway,' said Audrey, 'they didn't need anyone to act as guides, and the shop is salaried staff, so that just left committee-type things to do with fundraisings and suchlike.'

'But you'd be terrific at fundraising,' I said enthusiastically.

Audrey screwed up her nose. She knew I was lying. The closest Aud's ever come to raffles is staying in the hotel.

'Snithia offered me work keeping the books for the fundraising committee,' Audrey said scathingly. 'Apparently they've had sizeable donations recently and they're in an awful mess … and they haven't put in a tax return for years.'

'Oh,' I said, terribly disappointed for her, 'you can't do that sort of thing, can you?'

'No, I can't,' Audrey said, and a satisfied look crossed her face, 'but Tommy can. It's going to take him months.'

Isn't she a riot? You know life is good when there are people in the world who can still raise indolence to an art form. And you know life is better than good when you can race in from work, pour a drink, and have this next meal prepared in fifteen minutes.

Calamari à la Fish and Chip Shop

No, you're not ordering takeaway! Hoax Cuisine experts *never* have takeaway. And no, I haven't been struck by lightning.

You will need:

Oil for deep frying
1 packet frozen crumbed calamari rings
Lemon wedges
1 bottle tartare sauce

Method: Heat enough oil to cover calamari. When oil is hot, deep fry rings for three minutes, or until golden brown. Drain on absorbent paper.

Presentation: Pile calamari rings into a basket lined with an attractive serviette. Garnish with lots of fresh lemon wedges and serve with a healthy bowl of tartare sauce for dipping.

Note: There's no point in getting all sticky crumbing calamari yourself, especially when the supermarket freezer has done such a terrific job for you. The good brands are light, very tender, and cook in no time.

Smoked Rainbow Trout with Lemon and Horseradish

Smoked rainbow trout are already cooked when you buy them, so the fish is ready to eat, unless of course it's frozen! Smoked fish has a delicate flavour, and is an absolute must for your Hoax Cuisine portfolio. SRTs, as I call them, are expensive, so reserve them for special occasions, i.e. when everyone else is out. They are heaven eaten while sipping a Clare Valley Riesling.

You will need:

> Whole smoked rainbow trout (I buy them frozen from the
> supermarket. Allow one per person)
> Lemons, cut into wedges
> 1 jar horseradish cream
> Thin slices bread and butter
> Black pepper

Method: Defrost trout. Remove the fins and head and peel off the skin. Gently lift fillets off the bone on both sides.

Presentation: Place one or two fillets on a plate. Squeeze a little lemon juice over the fillets, and serve with a bowl of your 'homemade' horseradish cream, thin slices of bread and butter, lemon wedges and freshly grated black pepper.

Teriyaki Cutlets

What can I say? These delicious fish cutlets are as easy to make as they are to eat, and perfect for weekday dinners.

You will need:

> Fish cutlets (snapper, ling or jewfish), about 2cm thick
> 1 bottle teriyaki sauce
> 2–3 tablespoons peanut oil
> Fresh basil

Method: Marinade cutlets in teriyaki sauce for an hour, or however long it takes to have a bath and a glass of Australia's finest. Heat oil in a pan, drain cutlets and fry for a few minutes on each side until cooked.

Presentation: Place cutlets directly onto dinner plates and garnish with chopped fresh basil. These cutlets are also superb grilled or barbequed.

Crabs with Sweet Chilli Sauce

One of the most memorable meals I ever had was Maryland crabs
eaten at a kitchen table. There is something indescribably special
about laughing with good friends, sharing food from newspaper,
eating crabs with your fingers, and getting dirty fingerprints on
beer glasses. If you've done it, you'll know what I mean.

You will need:

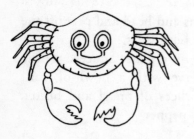

Cooked crabs
2 tablespoons peanut oil
2 garlic cloves, finely chopped
2 teaspoons grated or crushed ginger
¼ cup sweet chilli sauce
¼ cup tomato sauce
1 tablespoon soy sauce

Method: Remove body shell from crabs and discard gills, stomach
and fibrous tissue. Using a cleaver, chop crabs into four, leaving
legs on. Heat oil in a wok and fry garlic and ginger. Add all three
sauces and bring to boil. Add crabs and toss to cover in sauce.
Simmer gently for about three minutes.

Presentation: Tip crabs onto a large communal platter, give
everyone a glass of ice-cold beer and a serviette, and tuck in.

Kokoda

Pronounced 'Kokonda', this classic Fijian dish is perfect Hoax
Cuisine, as you don't have to cook it. The fish 'cooks' in the
marinade!

You will need:

½ kilo fresh white boneless fish (snapper, ling or barramundi)
Juice 4 limes (don't cheat with bottled cordial)
1 teaspoon salt
1 cup coconut cream

4 spring onions, finely sliced
1 green pepper, finely sliced
2 stalks celery, finely sliced
1 chilli, finely sliced
Fresh coriander for decoration

Method: Cut fish into bite-sized pieces, place in a glass bowl and marinate in lime juice and salt for a minimum of two hours. Remove fish from marinade, rinse under cold water, and drain well. Combine coconut cream, onions, green pepper, celery and chilli to taste. Add fish just before serving.

Presentation: I serve this in margarita glasses, decorated with a piece of coriander and a slice of lime. I'm so posh!

Fondue de la Pacifique

This is the easiest of meals to prepare, and as long as you make it look as though you made the sauces yourself, you can bask in glory! I usually transfer the sauces a couple of times so I have some dirty 'mixing bowls' in view.

You will need:

Ice cubes
Cooked prawns
Lemons
1 bottle tartare sauce
1 bottle seafood cocktail sauce

Method: Do not peel prawns! How hard was that?

Presentation: Place ice cubes in the bottom of a large bowl. Scatter prawns over ice. Cut lemons into wedges and scatter over prawns — don't squeeze them. Put the two sauces into separate bowls and place them on the table. Remember to place an empty bowl on the table for shells — these can be frozen until garbage day, or sent to your local member of parliament.

Letterbox Update

The postman is now involved. He has refused to deliver letters into a blue plastic bag hanging from the poinciana tree. I have taken his name and number, and informed him that mail is still being delivered in Ethiopia despite a lack of receptacles. He has told me he would very much like me to go there.

Chapter Five

Pasta and Pizza

Stop press. Dateline Roma Italia, April 1st 2000.
Record spaghetti crops harvested after recent rains;
agricultural minister to raise export quotas ...

Sorry, couldn't resist. It's the ultimate Hoax Cuisine, trotted out by cheeky European newspapers on April Fool's Day.

Pasta Tips

- Macaroni is the general term for all pasta.
- Pasta should be cooked in a large amount of rapidly boiling salted water.
- A few drops of olive oil added to boiling water will stop pasta from sticking.
- Fresh pasta cooks faster than dried.
- Pasta should be 'al dente': tender but firm.
- Never put soy sauce on pasta. Soy is for noodles.
- Cooked pasta can be reheated by soaking for two minutes in boiling water.
- The quality and taste of dried pasta varies enormously. It's up to you to experiment and find the one you like best.

Villa DiMaggio

- Wherever possible, use freshly grated parmesan cheese.
  And be seen doing it!

The Recipes

Here at Villa DiMaggio we eat vast quantities of pasta, primarily because the good quality sauces on the market lend themselves beautifully to Hoax Cuisine. Add a delicious chunk of parmesan from the deli, basil from your pot on the back step, and Roberto is your uncle.

My friend Jilly Salvatore is Irish, so naturally I approached her for a guest Italian pasta recipe. Jilly is a relief schoolteacher, married to a Sicilian. They have five children and two resident Asian students, which is why her recipe would have fed the Australian Olympic team. I've modified it for normal people.

Jilly Salvatore's
Extremely Easy Macaroni Cheesy

Very Italian so far!!!!
You will need:

200–250g pasta (rigatoni or penne)
1 bottle (approx. 2 cups) spinach and ricotta pasta sauce
(lots of different flavours on those shelves — experiment!)
Homemade breadcrumbs (whisk a chunk of crusty bread in the
blender)
Freshly grated parmesan cheese
Fresh chives

Method: Preheat oven to 180°C. Cook pasta in a large pan of
boiling salted water. Drain, and transfer to an oven dish. Pour
spinach and ricotta pasta sauce over pasta and mix gently. Sprinkle
top with breadcrumbs, parmesan, and chopped chives. Bake at
180°C for about 15 minutes.

Presentation: I swear this is what Jilly wrote: Place on table and
say, 'Eat that; it's good for you'. I should also add that one of her
part-Sicilian children had scrawled across the recipe in pencil:
'This tasty dish is traditionally served at gunpoint' ...

Jilly's Story

I'm not sure Jilly's got the hang of presenting Hoax Cuisine. Still,
it's a great recipe and I'm not game to complain, as Jilly doesn't
respond well to criticism. She's one tough cookie, a personality
trait not lost on those allocating classes to relief teaching staff.
Consequently she always lands the worst classes in school, a
situation that doesn't impress, but as work is scarce Jilly bites her
tongue.

There is one class Jilly teaches which is uncontrollable. We are
talking six-year-old barbarians: small people who steal lunch
money, scratch cars, vandalise other children's work, stick scissors

in live frogs, break windows, set fire to classrooms and pour water on computers. The regular class teacher ran away to join a circus.

Initially Jilly attempted to teach the class by sending unruly children outside, but stopped when she found herself alone in the classroom. There was also an unfortunate incident when Rory Kelly, aged six, took off up the Pacific Highway on the school ride-on mower. Jilly had her knuckles rapped. Should be more vigilant, that sort of thing.

The classroom that housed the crème de la crème of pre-pubescent savages had a small anteroom at one end, separated from the main room by a large window. It was intended for remedial reading, but Jilly used it for detentions. After the Rory incident she wasn't going to let a single child out of her sight. Her job, Jilly said, was to return a whole child with two arms and two legs to its parents at 3p.m.

Ten minutes into class time Jilly usually had a gathering of the same seven disruptive boys in the anteroom. She invented interesting things for them to do with cotton wool and empty egg cartons, and devised educational tasks that didn't involve sharp points or physical contact so she could teach the rest of the class.

To help retain her sanity Jilly also contrived a simple game that involved mentally renaming each child to suit his or her behaviour. She pinched the idea from the television show 'Gladiators' where terrific-looking humans with names like Flame and Storm contest their physical prowess. After all, the children called her Mrs Lavatory, and fair's fair.

And so it came to pass on the last Thursday before Father's Day 1998 Jilly had Torpor, Dormant, Gloom, Blur, Rank, Stiff and Fungi holed up in the anteroom making Father's Day cards. She had done the scissor part herself, and kept a wary eye on them while the other children learned about rainforests.

The boys were suspiciously quiet. It made Jilly nervous. Not one had fallen from the window. There were no bloodcurdling screams. Indeed, there was no blood. Jilly peered through the glass, certain they were creating hand grenades from felt-tip pens and cardboard. But they were sitting silently. It was extraordinary. Perhaps she had, at last, found something to interest them, even if it was only Father's Day cards. Or maybe they'd been at Blur's mother's pills again.

A short while later Kylie called out, 'Mrs Salvatore, Russel's crying.'

Jilly looked through the glass. Sure enough Gloom was weeping. And he wasn't alone. Rank and Dormant were whimpering, and Blur's bottom lip was trembling. Jilly didn't know about Fungi. She tried never to look at the spectacular vegetation growing from his nostrils.

Jilly opened the door, and asked warily, 'What's wrong?'

'Oh Miss,' stammered Fungi, 'Russel's father's in prison.'

'And Mum don't know where mine is, Miss,' cried Blur.

'And I haven't got one at all,' wailed Sniff.

'And I've got two and only one card,' sobbed Rank.

Jilly was devastated. Not for a moment had she considered this consequence of such a simple craft as making Father's Day cards. She promptly gathered up the materials and sat down, fought back her own tears, and read a Roald Dahl story to the boys. After lunch she bought them each an iceblock from the canteen, and reported the incident to the school councillor. Then she called in to see me on the way home and we roared with laughter until our stomachs hurt.

The first letter of complaint arrived on the principal's desk next morning: insensitive callous behaviour … not fit to teach children … an example must be made … picking on my son … thrown out of the profession. The usual invective.

By 3p.m. on Friday there were seven letters to the principal, seven to the Department of Education, and seven to the Minister for Education, all demanding Mrs Salvatore's removal from the school, teaching in general, and the face of the earth if possible.

'Bastards!' said the deputy principal, filing the letters away with the others, for not a single teacher in the school had been spared the wrath of these poisoned parental pens.

'I think perhaps,' continued the deputy, 'we might move you to 2S for the rest of the term.'

Jilly's heart soared. She was ecstatic. 2S were delightful. Thirty little angels. She pulled a glum face. It wouldn't do to appear elated. Or too keen.

'I shall miss them so much,' said Jilly. 'They were a challenging class.'

'It's for the best,' said the deputy supportively. 'These things happen. You mustn't take it personally.'

'I know,' murmured Jilly, nodding, and she smiled sadly.

The deputy patted her shoulder and said comfortingly, 'These parents and their vitriolic letters will never know the damage they do to a teacher's career.'

'No,' muttered Jilly, and she for one wasn't going to tell them.

Just for the record, Jilly calls me 'Scribble'. Very apt! Perhaps you'd like to play her name game at the dinner table while enjoying the following mouth-watering recipe. You can't use the name 'Crusty'. I've given it to our postman.

Lasagne

Everyone's favourite, and the safest meal to serve visiting dignitaries — i.e. 18-year-old foreign students touring Australia who stop to say hello and stay for a week. This happens when overseas friends' children take a year off before going to university, so be warned. They don't phone in advance, don't wash, don't help, don't have any money, and don't come alone. They will do Australia on your $5 a day.

I'm first to admit there is nothing as good as homemade lasagne, but for emergencies, such as above, it's hard to go past a frozen gourmet beef lasagne. There are, however, a few conditions attached, and I'm sorry to have to admit this Sara (big hint there), but I remove your lasagne from the tray, cut bits off the sides and corners, and force it into my own dish. Then I cover the top with homemade breadcrumbs and grated parmesan cheese before popping it in the oven. Oh, I feel so much better now I've told you.

While it's cooking we take bets on how many of our beers the visitors can drink before dinner. I tell you, they'll never use me on tourism ads.

Pasta Salad with Summer Peppers and Baby Mushrooms

This colourful salad may be served as a meal or accompaniment. It's important when using pasta in salad not to overcook the pasta, and to rinse it immediately in cold water to arrest the cooking process, otherwise it becomes floppy. So now you know.

You will need:

2 cups elbow pasta
½ cup marinaded sundried tomatoes (deli or bottled), drained and halved
1 red pepper, roughly chopped
1 green pepper, roughly chopped
1 cup baby button mushrooms
1 jar basil pesto
Fresh basil for garnish
A chunk of parmesan cheese

Method: Cook pasta in a large pan of boiling water. Rinse in cold water and drain well. Combine pasta, sundried tomatoes, red pepper, green pepper and baby mushrooms. Add basil pesto to personal taste. I use a full jar, but this may be too strong for you. Mix well.

Presentation: Serve in a large pasta bowl. Decorate with a central floret of fresh basil as this indicates you prepared the pesto yourself, and sprinkle with finely shaved parmesan cheese.

Note: Shave parmesan with either a potato peeler or steak knife — the latter makes attractive thin non-uniform shavings. There's nothing worse than chunks of plastic-looking cheese in a salad. The seventies have a lot to answer for.

Hot and Spicy Pizza

Nothing quite like homemade toppings on bought pizza bases for a quic and tasty Sunday evening supper. I tend to use what's left in the fridge, but if I've planned meals properly, and no one's pinched the ingredients, I find the following recipe a jolly good heart-starter for the week ahead.

You will need:

Thick pizza bases
Spicy pasta sauce
Shredded pizza cheese (allow 1 cup per pizza)
Large mushrooms, finely sliced
Sliced pepperoni (about 12 small slices per pizza)
Dried oregano
Kalamata olives (from the deli, not bottled)

Method: Place pizza base on a greased pizza pan, and prick all over with a fork. Spread about four tablespoons of spicy pasta sauce on base — not too much as you don't want it to get soggy. Sprinkle over half the cheese, then sliced mushrooms and pepperoni, and top with remaining cheese and a pinch of dried oregano. Remove pips from olives by pressing with base of a mug, halve and scatter over pizza. Bake in a hot oven (200°C) for about 20 minutes, or until crust is cooked.

If you have trouble cooking the base, or it remains doughy, slide pizza off the pan directly onto oven shelf five minutes before total cooking time.

Presentation: All good Hoax Cuisine cooks should have a pizza wheel for cutting pizza. Place pizza on a round wooden bread board and slice at the table. Quick slick rolls away from you are the best way to cut.

Fettuccine Carbonara

Yet another jewel from the Hoax Cuisine crown. This meal is perfect for those late suppers when you arrive home from the opera ...
You will need:

> Fettuccine pasta (I'll leave you to choose how much)
> 1 tub good quality carbonara or creamy bacon and mushroom
> sauce (from the supermarket fridge)
> Fresh coriander
> A Placido Domingo CD

Method: Cook fettuccine according to the packet instructions and drain well. Meanwhile heat the sauce in a pan, but do not boil. If you wish, fry some extra sliced mushrooms in butter and add to the sauce (and I mean butter, not margarine).
Presentation: Place pasta in a large bowl, pour over sauce, sprinkle with chopped fresh coriander, put on music, and dim the lights.

Señora Groff's Pizza Authentico

Naturally it would be asking for trouble to claim credit for a home-delivered pizza, but you can still keep the Hoax Cuisine ideal alive by announcing, 'This is fabulous, almost as good as mine'.
  I detest frozen pizza. Mostly I purchase ready-made pizza bases, though occasionally I make my own — you have no idea of the street credibility gained by a kid whose mum makes great pizza. The other advantage comes from a perception that it's difficult. I mean, would anyone doubt your other meals if you make pizza from scratch? If you don't wish to make dough, use the delicious topping on a bought base.
  For the base you will need:

> 1½ cups plain flour
> ½ teaspoon salt
> 1 teaspoon instant dried yeast (near the flour in supermarket)

½ teaspoon sugar
1 tablespoon good quality olive oil
150ml warm water

For the topping you will need:

4 tablespoons pasta sauce (choose an interesting flavour)
1 cup shredded pizza cheese
2 large mushrooms, finely sliced
¼ cup sliced red pepper
6 black olives (again I favour Kalamata)
½ tspn dried oregano

Method: Sift flour, salt and yeast into a large mixing bowl. Add sugar. Make a well in the middle and pour in oil and water. With one hand, work the ingredients together until you have a sticky ball — if you use both hands, the phone will ring. Turn onto a floured board and knead, adding flour as required, until it's no longer sticky. Form into a ball, pour a little olive oil onto your palm and rub gently over the dough. Transfer to a clean bowl and leave in a warm place for two hours, or until it's doubled in size.

When ready, place dough on a floured board, push it out with your hands to remove air and then roll into shape. This makes one large base. Place onto a greased pizza pan and prick all over with a fork. Spread sauce to edges and sprinkle half the cheese over it. Scatter on sliced mushrooms and red pepper, then top with remaining cheese, halved olives and dried oregano. Bake in a hot oven (200°C) for 20 minutes, or until crust is cooked.

Presentation: Transfer to a round bread board and slice at the table with a pizza wheel. Make sure preparation debris is visible and complain like crazy while washing up. You want to make the most of this. If nothing else, it will remind you of the value of Hoax Cuisine.

Ravioli with Sundried Tomatoes

There are squillions of variations on ravioli and sauce — the combinations of prepared products on offer are mind-boggling. This is my favourite, as it evokes fond memories of summer nights in Tuscany, eating under a loggia and sipping Chianti. At least it would if I'd been there.

You will need:

1 packet cheese and spinach ravioli
1 bottle sundried tomato pasta sauce
Freshly grated parmesan
Fresh coriander

Method: Cook ravioli according to the packet instructions. Drain well, and while still hot stir through enough sauce to suit personal taste. The cooler the ravioli, the less sauce will be absorbed by the pasta.

Presentation: Transfer to a large Italian-looking pasta bowl, and gently stir through parmesan and lots of chopped fresh coriander. Use basil if you prefer, but coriander has the edge. Another alternative is to scrap the parmesan and coriander, and garnish instead with coarsely grated lemon rind. This gives pasta a zesty kick — similar to preserved lemons, all the rage in Melbourne dontcha know.

Letterbox Update

The fallen bricks that I piled neatly by the drive ready for reconstruction have been stolen. I am reviewing my stand on the death penalty. There has been a suggestion from other senior management that I would enjoy a new, state of the art letterbox for my birthday present. Yeah, right.

Chapter Six

Meals with Meat

Never eat more than you can lift.

— MISS PIGGY

Personally speaking I never *lift* anything over five kilos unless it's fallen off a bicycle, and I never *eat* anything unless I know exactly what's in it. This last phobia dates back to childhood and suspicious jars of mincemeat my mother purchased to make Christmas mince pies. I imagined all manner of body parts mashed into the unattractive black and cream concoction. I can still see little minces, small and sleek like ferrets, tearing out of our woods across the water meadows, hotly pursued by axe-wielding furriers and butchers. I can, truly I can.

Meat Tips

- The more expensive the meat, the less time it takes to cook.
- Fat-free beef is tasteless.
- Grilled meat is easier to digest than fried (useful to know if you happen to be preparing lunch at the bowls club).

- Roast meat should be 'stood' outside the oven for 20 minutes before carving.
- Ham carved off the bone by your butcher is light years ahead of processed products.
- When trainee gourmands turn up collective noses at 'rare' roast meat, cut off a few slices and lightly grill them — the meat, not the children.
- Be loyal to your butcher. You will be rewarded with quality cuts and valuable information on important meat issues, such as where to get a pink slip for your rusty 20-year-old banger.

The Recipes

I have to report a serious oversight in the time-saving meat recipes offered at supermarkets — there's too much standing around stirring when the cook could be getting on with a stiff drink and a sit-down. Yes ladies, minimum preparation time, an hour or so with a cheeky red from the Hunter Valley, and a finale of domestic adulation can be yours with that quintessential pioneer of time-saving cookery, the humble roast! That's a tip, by the way.

My guest recipe for this chapter is down-home southern fare from Veronica, a West Indian lady whom I haven't seen for thirty years. Like roast it doesn't require constant receptacle attendance and, like Veronica, it's heart-warming and easy. It was perfect for my heady student days of one-gas-ring cookery, and has stood me in good stead on many sailing holidays. You won't get wows if emerging from a regular kitchen with this meal, but it's an impressive and delicious offering from a pot over a campfire. The golden rule is location, location, location.

Veronica's Southern Soul Casserole

You will need:

2 tablespoons olive oil
1 onion, chopped
½ kg minced beef
1 x 250ml box beef stock
1 cup tomato pasta sauce (choose one with herbs)
2 celery stalks, sliced
1 x 270g can corn kernels, drained
1 x 425g can whole new potatoes, drained
1 x 410g can whole baby carrots, drained
2 teaspoons dried thyme
1 tablespoon Worcestershire Sauce
Black pepper

Method: Heat oil in a heavy-based saucepan. Fry onion and mince until meat is browned. Add everything else in the above order. Mix well and simmer on lowest heat possible for 30 minutes, stirring between drinks to prevent sticking.

Presentation: Ladle into bowls and serve with fresh damper from the bakery. Yes, I agree, pretending you made the damper is a fine idea. Good to see you're getting the hang of Hoax Cuisine.

A brief footnote: I recently sat next to a Louisiana dentist named Bubba on a bus ride between the LC-39 observation gantry and the Vehicle Assembly Building at Kennedy Space Centre. We were both there to see the launch of the space shuttle Atlantis.

He was eating enthusiastically from a flask, and the contents smelt and looked like Veronica's casserole. I was not surprised

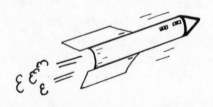

when Bubba informed me it was his Mammy's authentic southern casserole, full of big ole carrots, suckers from a can, and other things Veronica. In honour of the coincidence we made a pinkie wish and, if you're reading this book, mine came true.

Just for the record they cancelled the shuttle launch. I made two more futile attempts but each time Houston had a problem. I referred to my 'must do in America' list and settled instead for parking a Chevy on the levee. Mad, eh?

Veronica's Story

I first met Veronica in 1973 when, as part of my obstetrics nurse training, I was sent to educate mothers at an antenatal clinic on a housing estate in South London. It was the sort of place you see on British cop shows with boarded windows and injured bodies on seedy stairwells. Time has moved on and it's now a trendy warehouse conversion full of men called Nigel who say 'absolutely' a lot.

Much to everyone's amusement I had drawn the short straw of antenatal clinics, my own fault as I was off sick the day placements were made, probably with glandular fever or a picnic in Kew Gardens.

I viewed this impending appointment with a certain amount of fortitude and took to hanging around the infectious diseases ward in the hope of catching something nasty that wouldn't scar, but would take approximately three months to cure. In desperation I telephoned the Common Cold Research Centre to see if they wanted to squirt a noxious substance up my nose. They declined, informing me they had a full quota of Cambridge students, so I took a number 12 bus from depot to depot and sat upstairs and breathed deeply the cigarette and bronchitis fumes. It was no use. I was immune to every germ south of Watford Gap.

I watched enviously as friends cycled off to their safe and comfortable antenatal clinics, and I hoped they would enjoy themselves and learn a lot, and that one of them would fall off her bicycle and break her neck so I could replace her.

For my part I cycled to and from my clinic every day, a distance of eight miles each way. My journey took me through a London suburb called Elephant and Castle and I always made a slight detour past a car wrecker called The Elephant Repair Centre, just so I could have one laugh a day. This was, in retrospect, one of the highlights of my training. Sometimes after a few gins one of the nurses would telephone from the nurses' home and ask if they could fix our elephant. We certainly knew how to enjoy ourselves in those days.

The mothers at the clinic hated me. I was young, blonde, unmarried, owned a bicycle and wasn't pregnant: the complete escape inventory. I smiled a lot and said really nice things about their hair and, by the end of the second day, I felt they were warming to me as I had earned the nickname, 'effing white honky'.

For the most part they completely ignored me and sat on the floor discussing Sunday visits to Brixton prison, or compared tattoos and tuna fish recipes while I ponced around up the front with a pointy stick and a chart. I tried to join in with stories of prisons I had visited, like Alcatraz, and I even showed them my appendix scar but they continued to treat me like dog-do.

On day three the senior midwife withdrew me from the birth classes because, as she so nicely phrased it, I had lost control of the room. And so it was I found myself on a rubber mat in front of twenty very pregnant ladies performing a sort of gym-elastics, or as the noticeboard called it, daily exercise classes.

We were not a pretty sight. I was thin as a whip. They were taller when they were lying down. They hated me even more. I was now the effing evil white honky.

'Stretch those legs,' I'd call.

'Swing those arms,' I'd sing.

'Oh sod off,' they'd yell.

I tell you, never in human history has so little been learnt by so few from no one.

Then Veronica arrived, a large West Indian woman having her ninth child, so she needed me, like, really a lot. I loved her. She called me Nurse Honky. She was always smiling. Always laughing. And boy, could she laugh. Her whole body would shake like blancmange and she'd fold her arms under humungous breasts and shake those too, and then tears would roll down her plump round face and she'd fall to the ground and laugh and laugh as she slammed the floor with her fists and shouted, 'O Lordy Lordy'. Sometimes the whole show would take five minutes, but at other times Veronica could go from nought to 'O Lordy, Lordy' in ten seconds.

I became hostage to Veronica's good humour and tended to direct my words and demonstrations towards her. One day I had positioned the mothers on their hands and knees and was teaching them to swing their behinds from side to side and turn their heads at the same time, an exercise designed to strengthen the spine during pregnancy.

'Come on Veronica,' I chirped, 'bend that lovely bottom to the side and turn that head.'

'O Lordy Lordy, Nurse Honky,' said Veronica, 'It's doing this that got me here in the first place.'

We collapsed. All of us. And we laughed and cried and rolled around on the floor, and some of us, in honour of Veronica, beat out 'O Lordy Lordy' on the linoleum like it was a crazy Lamaze breathing technique.

This is the scene that greeted the senior nurse tutor who had come to do my interim assessment.

'May I see you outside?' she said.

I jumped up and wiped my eyes with a towel, and as I left the room remarked flippantly over my shoulder, 'Take a rest, girls'. It was a very professional moment.

'I must say,' said the nurse tutor, 'you seem to have struck a chord with these mothers and I will make reference to this in my report. It's usual practice to move nurses from difficult clinics after a few weeks, but as you are doing so well I have decided to leave you. Well done, Nurse Groff.'

This is the only moment in my life when I have been filled with pride and horrified at the same time. It was not a good feeling, but it disappeared as quickly as it came.

I returned to class to find the mothers lying on the floor smoking and telling a dirty joke that involved Nurse Honky's small chest size. I wasn't bothered. I had succeeded where others had failed. I was practically a career.

Glowing with pride I stood up the front, and with a smile from ear to ear, I exercised like a mad woman while my charges remained floor-bound and puffed away and told jokes. I didn't care. I was getting fit. I was getting a good report. It would make up for that unfortunate incident after the nurses' ball when someone in London painted red paw prints over a bridge, all the way to the South Bank lion.

Well, thank heavens for Veronica. It's doubtful I would have passed my nursing finals without that glowing report, and who knows what would have happened if I hadn't made a pinkie wish with Bubba.

On with the show and another brilliant Hoax Cuisine recipe. How does she do it?

Shepherds' Thighs with Fresh Rosemary

This is our family name for mouth-watering lamb cutlets, so called because, when artistically designed on a plate, they resemble a pair of legs. Served with a huge green salad and crusty French bread, they're perfect for Sunday lunch, a summer evening at 'ome, or a barbeque. Children love them, so you always need more than you think (yes, the lamb — you're such a card!).

You will need:

Lamb cutlets — extra trim or French cut
1 bottle mustard, honey and herb marinade
A few sprigs fresh rosemary

Method: Baste cutlets on both sides with some of the marinade and grill or barbeque until meat is just pink in the middle. This cut of meat is very tender, so there is no need to marinade for any length of time.

Presentation: Arrange cutlets on a serving dish and garnish with sprigs of fresh rosemary.

Chicken Tikka Masala à la Maggie

This is a medium strength Rajasthani curry with which I have taken great liberties. It has a delicate fruity flavour and isn't too hot for children. If young ones start to bleat, stir through some cream or natural yoghurt at the end to cool things down a bit.

You will need:

2 tablespoons olive oil
1 red onion, chopped
500g chicken breast fillet, sliced into bite-sized pieces
1 apple, peeled, cored and sliced
1 can tikka masala cooking sauce (there are several good brands in the supermarket. If you use tikka masala paste, follow jar instructions or mix ⅓ cup of paste with 150ml boiling water)
½ cup apple juice
½ cup sultanas
½ cup water
Fresh coriander

Method: Heat oil in a heavy saucepan and fry onion and chicken for about five minutes. Add apple and fry for a few minutes. Add tikka masala sauce, apple juice, sultanas and water. Simmer very gently, covered, for about an hour. Stir through a little more water if liquid has reduced too much, and just before serving, add chopped fresh coriander.

Presentation: Family traditions, family traditions. My paternal grandparents were rubber planters in Malaya where curry and rice was served at their bungalow in separate elegant bowls. On the other hand my Ugandan Asian relatives put curry on top of rice in a similar elegant bowl, and scoop it up with Indian bread. In order to remain bipartisan I arrange rice in a circle on a dinner plate and spoon curry into the middle. As you don't have the curry nazis breathing down your neck you can do as you wish.

A Poke in the Pig

Otherwise known as pork satays. Great name, isn't it? Hard to believe no one's thought of it before! Incidentally, if you're still making satay sauce from scratch, you need to get out more.

You will need:

Pork fillet
Wooden kebab sticks
1 bottle satay sauce (lots of good brands out there!)
Fresh coriander

Method: Cut pork fillet into thin slices and thread onto kebab sticks. Place in a single layer in a flat dish and brush with lashings of satay sauce. Barbeque or grill for a few minutes on each side, basting frequently with sauce until cooked.
Presentation: Place satays on an attractive platter and sprinkle over some finely chopped fresh coriander.

Laughing Stock Stroganoff

Yes, beef stroganoff made entirely from cattle with a sense of humour. At least I hope so. The quality of meat used is the keynote to success with this recipe — don't even think of cheating with pre-cut stir-fry beef — it'll turn this beautiful dish into cardboard stroganoff.

You will need:

500g top quality steak (Porterhouse, New York cut, etc)
2 tablespoons olive oil
1 bottle good quality stroganoff sauce (approximately 2 cups.
There are several bottled brands on the supermarket shelf
— don't use packet mixes)

Method: Slice steak diagonally into thin strips. Heat oil and seal steak strips quickly on the outside. Drain off fat and leave meat to stand while you heat the stroganoff sauce. Drain meat again, add to sauce, and heat through. Do not overcook — the less cooking, the more tender the beef.

Presentation: No need for decoration — this dish is perfect on its own. Serve with rice, salad and sourdough bread.

Jay Groff's Chilli

I have included this recipe because, for me, it's real Hoax Cuisine. You see, I don't make it at all, my husband does. I have been as faithful as possible to the method he employs, and I expect if your partner prepares this meal, it will not be dissimilar.

You will need:

1 onion
1 red pepper
2 cloves garlic
2 tablespoons olive oil
½ kilo minced beef
1 chilli, finely chopped
1 x 415g can tomatoes
1 x 440g can kidney beans
1 teaspoon dried oregano

Method: Peel and finely chop onion, red pepper and garlic, throwing peelings into sink. Heat oil and cook onion, red pepper and minced beef until meat is browned. Add garlic and remaining ingredients, taking care to dribble some of the tomato down front of stove. Meanwhile tread spilt pieces of onion into cork floor. Stir thoroughly, cover and simmer gently for 30 minutes. Check regularly, making sure you drip mixture over stovetop when lifting lid. When cooked inform someone you have cooked dinner and disappear to Golf Club.

Presentation: Ladle chilli into bowls and serve with chunks of fresh cob bread. Announce 'I love this' four times throughout meal.

Sound familiar? Thought so. Still, it's a great meal, and a good recipe to teach children to cook, as it's almost impossible to ruin. Unlike your kitchen!

Hog Heaven in Sauerkraut

My apologies to Miss Piggy for including this classic European dish, but it's so easy and delicious I couldn't possibly leave it out.
  You will need:

Pork loin chops
2 tablespoons olive oil
1 can sauerkraut
A little water

Method: Remove excess fat from chops. Heat oil in a large frying pan and brown pork on both sides. Drain off fat and spread sauerkraut over the pork (some cans may be dry — if so, add a little water). Cover pan and simmer gently for about 45 minutes, or until meat begins to fall off the bone, or your bathwater gets cold, whichever comes first.
Presentation: You don't want to interfere with the subtle flavours, so no throwing greenery on top. However, because this dish is bland in colour, I suggest you serve it with bright vegetables such as steamed green beans sprinkled with lemon juice.

A cautionary word: I should advise these ingredients might produce a combination of noxious gases — my secret weapon at Thursday night tennis for years.

Letterbox Update

Guess what? Crusty the Postman's on stress leave. His replacement is a pleasant woman who is quite happy with the blue plastic bag in the poinciana tree arrangement. She doesn't know what's wrong with Crusty, but she's certain it's not a human disease because everyone knows he's a pig. I think she's on to something there. No news on the stolen bricks. They're probably in Victoria by now.

Chapter Seven

Vegetables

I am not a vegetarian because I love animals.
I am a vegetarian because I hate plants.

I don't know who originally said this but it makes me laugh each time I read it. And no, I'm not vegetarian. I have pointy canines and I'm not afraid to use them.

You may find this difficult to believe but I remember eating my first banana — and my first choko. Born in England after the war, I was subject to the joys of food rationing, so it was a red-letter day when Tom Saunders drove his old vegetable truck up Edward Grove and the whole street turned out to view his bananas. Mum purchased three, and this considerably increased our social standing in Portchester. I was five years old and proud as hell to have a mother who bought foreign food.

I was a little older and in a different country when I had my first choko. Or it had me. Whoever introduced this vegetable to the Australian mainland should be shot at sunrise. The only way to cook it is to boil the choko in lightly salted water for 15 minutes, drain well, wrap in foil, and then throw away.

Vegetable Tips

- Purchase fresh produce in season. It's cheaper and the flavour is better.
- Purchase a rabbit. They are connoisseurs of vegetable quality, and greenies will stop pestering you to establish a compost heap.

The Recipes

It's not always necessary or possible to take shortcuts with vegetables, as for the most part fresh and natural is best. Hoax Cuisiners should therefore view vegetable preparation as an opportunity to advertise culinary ability, and there's no better way to do this than preparing ordinary vegetables in unusual ways, and unusual vegetables in ordinary ways.

With this paradox in mind I asked my vegetarian friend Annie for a guest recipe. Annie knows her onions, and as expected her beautifully handwritten instructions for grilled aubergines were on my kitchen table first thing Monday morning. She also has a ripper story to tell — let me just say Annie is a member of an exclusive club with the smallest membership in the world. Bet that's got your antenna waggling!

Annie Ramsey's Grilled Aubergine Teriyaki

Aubergines, otherwise known as eggplant or purple doovers, are a terrific vegetable for Hoax Cuisine cooks because apart from throwing them in a ratatouille, not many people know what to do with them so they'll be impressed just by your using them.

You will need:

Firm baby aubergines
Olive oil
1 bottle good quality teriyaki marinade or sauce

Method: Wash and dry aubergines, remove stem, and cut lengthways into ½cm thick slices. Brush both sides with olive oil. Pour some teriyaki marinade into a saucer (I do love finding uses for saucers) and brush aubergine slices liberally with the marinade. Place under a hot grill and, basting frequently with more marinade, cook for five minutes on each side, or until slices are soft and slightly charred.

Presentation: Pile grilled aubergine slices onto an attractive platter and serve immediately. Annie might not appreciate my carnivorous interference with her recipe, but grilled aubergines are splendid with roast pork.

Annie's Story

I was right. Annie got all thingy about the meat and demanded creative control of her story — a huge advantage for me as she has total recall as well as, how shall I put it, a permanent memento of the occasion.

We have to trawl back thirty years to Annie's first pregnancy. She was, you know, very herbal about the whole thing and paraded around in enormous billowy dresses, stomach to the fore like a ship under sail, grinning like the Cheshire Cat at buildings and furniture. If she'd had a tail she'd have wagged it.

Not for Annie the drugs and pain-relieving back rubs. None of that. She was going to be strong. Memorable. A peasant squatting in a field. Well, almost. Annie's over the top when it comes to personal expectations.

She imagined herself giving birth while reading the paper, perhaps sipping a martini, then causing great mirth in the delivery room by remarking, 'Was that *all* there was to it?' Doctors and nurses would shake their heads at such unassailable magnificence and talk about her in the staff canteen for weeks. Annie glowed with anticipation. She was going to be a mother in a million. Just like the rest of us.

April Fool's day dawned dark and foreboding with rain salting freshly cleaned windows and wind rattling doors. Undeterred by nature's misery, Annie relined the kitchen drawers with old wallpaper, arranged tinned food in alphabetical order in the pantry, and made a note of things to replenish. She was bending over to retrieve a smelly old potato that had rolled under the wine rack when a violent clenching pain shot through her belly. She sat on the floor winded. Nothing to worry about, Annie thought. A Braxton Hicks contraction. This can happen in late pregnancy. Annie knew.

But the pain came again. And again. Visions of lying in hospital, an unwilling victim of the dreaded salmonella virus, flashed through her mind. Or even a burst appendix. Anything, Annie said, to suppress the fearful reality. The baby wasn't due for six weeks. She was the perfect mother who'd done all the right things. Godammit, she'd even got the haemorrhoids.

Annie doesn't recall arriving at the hospital. She has a vague memory of flashing lights, trays of silver duck-billed speculums, and a pasty-looking man in a white coat leaning over and saying 'I'm going to take your baby away.'

Annie thinks she screamed. Somehow Peter her husband was there, white-faced and trembling.

'It's dead, isn't it?' cried Annie, 'Oh my God, someone tell me it's not dead.'

'He's not,' said the nurse, trying to smile, but not too much as things weren't that good.

A son. Annie and Peter had a son.

Annie said her heart was torn to pieces, her whole being seized by an unearthly loss, so desperate was she to touch and kiss the tiny dark form that had slithered from her loins.

The doctor reappeared looking sombre and when he spoke Annie told me his words seemed to come from far away.

'Your son is six weeks premature,' he said, and Annie recalls him placing a comforting hand on Peter's shoulder. 'He is very weak. We are doing everything we can.'

Annie and Peter clung to each other and cried: great heart-wrenching sobs that reverberated round cold clinical walls. Annie was sedated and drifted in and out of consciousness while the nasty business with the placenta was dealt with.

An eternity later they were taken to a room full of lights and machines and charts and tubes. A nurse shuffled them over to an oxygen tent in the corner. Someone had written 'Baby Ramsey' on the label. They stared in horror at the frail scrawny body in the plastic bubble, his chest flinching in small jerky movements like a frog in a ghastly school experiment.

'His name's Christopher,' Annie said accusingly to the nurse, 'Christopher Ramsey,' and Peter stared sympathetically at Annie while a silent tear snaked down his cheek.

A few days later the hospital discharged Annie but she refused to leave, and much to the doctors' and nurses' annoyance, and totally against hospital policy, insisted on sleeping on a metal camp bed in the nurses' tearoom. Peter, secretly impressed by Annie's stand, trudged to and from home with food and clean clothes, and resigned himself to the inadequate visiting hours.

They took photos. They watched and they loved. Tears and smiles. Love and guilt. Hope and heartbreak.

Things looked bleak for a while as Christopher initially failed to thrive, but Annie said she never wavered from her knowing. She was positive he would survive, and with every positive thought and action it was as if she was infusing strength into her child by a sort of remote maternal osmosis.

Of course Annie was right. Peter has often said they should be called Mr and Mrs Right, and Annie should be renamed 'Always'. Christopher started to gain weight, gram by gram, and slowly the tubes were removed, one by one. Annie gathered application forms from schools and planned Christopher's life as far as practicality would allow. Peter watched in silence.

At five weeks Annie held her son for the first time. Christopher snuggled close and the nurse practically had to get Annie in a headlock to return Christopher to his cot. Their little man went from strength to strength. He smiled at Annie. But it wasn't an ordinary smile. Tiny gold flecks danced in his cobalt blue eyes and the edges of his rosebud mouth quivered precariously. Annie fell hopelessly in love: an uncomplicated, undemanding and uncritical love that frightened her. Annie hadn't known herself capable of such feelings and was consumed by this newly discovered awareness.

When Christopher was three months old he was discharged from hospital. Annie and Peter were both nervous, but listened intently as the nurse explained Christopher might have trouble sleeping as he was used to noise and bright lights. Why didn't she shut up? What did Annie care if he screamed day and night? He was going *home*. They had beaten the cruel trick of nature. They had won. She hadn't spent three months on that lumpy camp bed in the nurses' tearoom for nothing!

But nature, it seems, had one more trick to play on Mr and Mrs Right.

As tradition demands, Annie stood on the steps of the hospital holding her son while Peter took the obligatory photograph. A gentle breeze blew Christopher's wispy dark hair and Annie licked her fingers and smoothed it down just as Peter clicked the camera.

It made a wonderful natural picture. Wonderful because it contained one mother and two babies, one precious bundle in Annie's arms, and a smaller more delicate cargo in her belly. It still stands in a silver frame on the piano in Annie's sunroom, although time has faded the colours. Annie adores it when people ask about the photograph.

'Yes,' she says, 'Christopher was so little the day we came home from hospital,' and she pauses for a moment before adding mischievously, 'and so was April!'

Shocking behaviour, isn't it? I blame vegetables, even if I have benefited enormously from Annie's vegan qualifications. Lucky for me she managed to take time out from having it off in nurses' tearooms, and show me how to cook and eat artichokes. Like many people I had been ignorant and yes, nervous, of an artichoke's modus operandi (also known to the more experienced as MO).

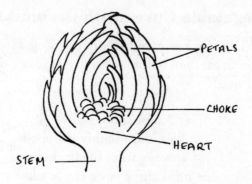

CROSS-SECTION of ARTICHOKE

Artichauts au Naturel

There's nothing like an artichoke to consolidate Hoax Cuisine cooking credentials. Truly the aristocrat of finger foods, this sublime vegetable is a must for your table.

You will need:

Artichokes
Melted butter

Method: Choose artichokes with tightly packed leaves, and wash well under cold running water. Pull off lower outer petals and trim stem. You can level off tips of petals with scissors if you wish, but I don't bother. Cook in boiling salted water for 25 to 40 minutes, until artichoke is tender and petals pull out easily from centre. Drain well. Ease back centre leaves and remove choke (the fibrous fuzzy flower), taking care not to scrape away any of the heart just below.

Presentation: To eat, pull off a petal by the tip, dip in melted butter, place in your mouth, and pull between teeth, scraping the length of the petal. Then discard the petal. When you have scraped them all, you will be left with the coup de grâce, the artichoke heart, which is easiest to eat with a knife and fork. *Splendid MO, don't you think? Book 'im Danno!*

Vegetable Curry with Coconut Cream

This mild curry is a wonderful way of using winter vegetables. It takes longer to eat than it does to prepare. Hoax Cuisine at its finest! You will need:

2 tablespoons olive oil
1 onion, roughly chopped
4 cloves garlic, finely chopped
2 tablespoons mild curry paste (I use tikka masala paste)
1 x 400ml can coconut cream
½ cup yoghurt (natural or vanilla)
½ cup tomato paste (or pasta sauce)
1 large potato, scrubbed and cubed
1 cup broccoli, divided into 'green trees'
1 cup cauliflower, divided into 'white trees'
1 cup celery, sliced
1 cup button mushrooms
Fresh coriander

Method: Heat oil in a large pan and fry onion and garlic until soft. Add curry paste and fry for one minute. Add coconut cream, yoghurt, and tomato paste. Bring to the boil and add potato. Simmer very gently on lowest heat possible for ten minutes. Add remaining vegetables and simmer for five to ten more minutes until all vegetables are cooked. Remove from heat and stir through chopped fresh coriander.

Presentation: Try to leave the pan standing for at least an hour to let coriander pervade the curry. Reheat gently and serve with rice.

Mushroom Tapas

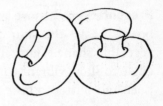

Tapas originated in Spain and have fast become a fun food trend. Quite simply, 'tapas' is the name given to little side dishes of food served in tapas bars. They can be anything from deep fried nibbles to interesting vegetable treats. They may be eaten alone, as a meal accompaniment, or with little biscotti.

You will need:

2–4 tablespoons butter
2 cups small button mushrooms
1 clove garlic, finely chopped
2 tablespoons balsamic vinegar
Fresh basil

Method: Heat butter and when hot, fry mushrooms until tender. Add chopped garlic and toss. Pour balsamic vinegar over mushrooms and cook for two more minutes. Remove from heat and stir through chopped fresh basil.

Presentation: Tapas seem to be served in white dishes, so I guess we should follow tradition. This recipe also makes a pleasant topping for toast.

Baked Sweet Potato with Lemon

One of the most visually appealing and satisfying vegetables to cook is a baked sweet potato in its jacket.

You will need:

A large sweet potato as uniform in shape as possible
1 lemon
Butter

Method: Scrub potato and prick it at both ends. Wrap in double foil and bake at 180°C for one and a half hours, or longer if sweet potato is very large.

Presentation: Remove sweet potato from foil and place on a bread board. Leave the skin on and cut into slices, retaining overall vegetable shape. Transfer carefully to a platter and lay slices at an angle to show vibrant colour to its best advantage. Top with lemon juice and butter to taste.

Hoax Raclette with New Potatoes

A favourite memory of living in Switzerland was driving to the Refuge de Friance in the mountains above Montreux, and eating raclette by an open fire. Great wheels of local cheese were halved, positioned on the raclette in the fireplace, and as the cheese melted it was scooped onto cooked potatoes. Groff piggies consumed helpings at an alarming rate, and on returning to Australia and no fireplace, I adopted a more 'domestic' approach to this traditional Swiss cookery.

You will need:

Small new potatoes
Gruyère cheese
Freshly grated black pepper
1 jar dill pickles (optional)

Method: Steam new potatoes until cooked, allow to cool to just warm, and place, close together, in a single layer in a fireproof dish. Lay thin slices of gruyère over the potatoes. Cook under a hot grill until cheese oozes over potatoes.
Presentation: Grate black pepper over potatoes, place dish on the table and let everyone dig in. This is a 'no standing on ceremony meal', and wonderful served with a side dish of dill pickles.

Lotus Blossom Onion

My vegetable finale is a flamboyant way of preparing onions. This recipe is sweeping the United States, knocking buffalo wings (an American fried chicken wing recipe from Buffalo, New York) off the best-seller list, and Hoax Cuisine cooks need to know all about it. It takes a few goes to perfect the cutting, but once you've grasped the technique you'll be amazed at the spectacular results. It took me two goes and two bandaids to get it right.

Americans use large sweet onions, but these are difficult to find in Australia, so until grocers catch on you will have to contend with any large onions. Bloomin' onions, as they are known stateside, are now so popular in US restaurants that Wal-Mart sells a special gizmo to do the cutting for you!

You will need:

Large onions (preferably sweet)
Plain flour
1 x 150g packet instant batter mix
Water
Vegetable oil for deep-frying
Lettuce leaves
1 bottle blue cheese dressing (a creamy European dressing from
the supermarket fridge)

Method: Peel onion, leaving root end intact. Slice off the top and, taking care not to cut through the root, cut downwards from top into 16 equal segments. Plunge onion into boiling water for one minute, then iced water for five minutes. Drain well, cut side down. Gently ease apart the petals so onion resembles a lotus blossom. Place onion and enough flour to coat in a plastic bag and shake gently. Mix instant batter with water as specified on packet, whisking for one minute. Dip floured onion into batter and coat thoroughly. Place on a plate, cut side up, and chill in the fridge for at least one hour. Heat oil and deep fry onion until golden brown, turning as necessary. Drain on paper towels.
Presentation: I serve one onion to each guest. Line a soup dish with lettuce leaves, and arrange your Lotus Blossom Onion on top. To eat, pluck off an onion petal and dip it into the blue cheese dressing. Finger food at its best.

Lotus Blossom Onion

Letterbox Update

In our street we have two seasons, summer and construction. As it's now summer there will be no manly mixing of concrete until the grass stops growing. We have, however, bought new bricks, appropriately stressed, and these are safely hidden in our garage ready for action. Just like the exercise bike.

Crusty has returned to work and remains steadfast in his refusal to deposit letters in the blue plastic bag. A neighbour has kindly given us an old metal milk churn to use as a letterbox. My husband has wedged it securely in a crook of the poinciana tree. I do think, in the interests of compromise, he could have positioned the milk churn lower down ...

Chapter Eight

Salads

*'It is said that the effect of eating too much
lettuce is soporific.'*

So said Beatrix Potter in her *Tale of the Flopsy Bunnies* published in
1909. The good news is that recent research has shown Miss
Potter's garden observations to be correct, and too much lettuce
does indeed cause excessive drowsiness. The bad news is it only
works on rabbits, not children.

Salad Tips

- Be adventurous. Salad leaves, sold by the kilo, are an easy
  way of purchasing a variety of lettuce. Baby spinach,
  usually sold in bags, is also a fabulous salad base. And
  don't forget rocket, the leafy flavour of the month, which
  has a delicious peppery flavour.
- Experiment with salad dressings. There are a squillion
  different products out there made from herbs and spice
  and all things nice. It's also important to memorise salad
  dressing quantities so you can whip some up in front of
  guests while talking about world issues (the recipe is on
  page 121 of my other book *Mothers Behaving Badly*).

- Rub the inside of salad bowls with cut garlic. This has the same effect as the old barman's trick of upending a drinking glass in a tray of gin — the concentration of flavour on the rim makes a gin and tonic taste really strong.
- Instead of a traditional salad, serve a platter of freshly cut vegetables in season with a gourmet dip such as guacamole, hummus, or taramasalata (transferred into your own container, of course).
- Don't forget an extra salad is a great meal extender if more guests appear at the table. My favourite emergency salad dish is a bowl of whole beetroots (two large cans). Delicious, colourful, and no effort at all.

The Recipes

My little black Netherlands dwarf rabbit has just fallen asleep on the rug beside my desk. I don't need to smell his breath. I know he has been up the road eating my friend Poppy's lettuces. After this nap he'll hop back and dig up Poppy's radishes before snacking at the celery patch.

Poppy loves him and will not use fertilisers in case it upsets Flopsy's tum. She told me he eats in order. Lettuce, radish, celery, carrot top, parsley, basil, spinach. Then he runs clear over her field, tossing hither and high in the long grass before arriving home to take up his begging position beside our fridge, nose pressed against the door seal.

Who else but Poppy could I possibly have asked for a guest salad recipe?

Poppy's Asian Fried Noodle Salad with Lemon Soy Dressing

Poppy has been making this zingy salad for picnics and parties since I don't know when, and it's a real crowd-pleaser. I make it when the price of lettuce goes sky high: sort of biting my thumb at the establishment.

You will need:

½ Chinese cabbage, washed and thinly sliced
5 or 6 spring onions, chopped
1 cup baby mushrooms, thinly sliced
½ cup slivered almonds, toasted until golden brown
¼ cup olive oil
¼ cup fresh lemon juice
2 teaspoons sugar
1 tablespoon soy sauce
1 tablespoon chopped fresh chives
1 x 100g packet pre-cooked fried noodles

Method: Put Chinese cabbage, spring onions, mushrooms and almonds into a salad bowl. Blend together olive oil, lemon juice, sugar, soy sauce and chives and pour over salad. Toss well.
Presentation: Just before serving, stir-fried noodles through salad.

Memo from Poppy: Rabbits do not like salad dressing on this recipe!

Poppy's Story

A big thank you to Poppy for enhancing my Hoax Cuisine collection of salad dishes. And a big thank you to her for feeding my errant rabbit. It sounds crazy but over the years he has probably spent as much time in Poppy's garden as I have in her kitchen, and believe me, I've spent a lot of time in Poppy's kitchen. Our relationship has never been one of those sit down over coffee deals. One of us is always fixing something or preparing meals, and the other chips in. It works well.

Life has been a struggle for Poppy. Her husband died ten years ago and she has single-handedly put two sons through school and juggled economic constraint, adolescent demands, and menopausal hormones. The full catastrophe.

'Bloody Robert,' Poppy said to me one day, 'bloody Robert and his bloody little insurance policy.' She picked up a King George V letter opener and began to spread butter with it (yes, even Poppy wouldn't dare use margarine in my presence). It was one of Robert's personal treasures, given him by his godfather. Poppy used it in the kitchen because she was cross with Robert for dying and leaving her poor. Her 'angry' period, the grief counsellor called it. 'Don't worry; it won't last long,' the counsellor had said.

'Shows how much they know,' said Poppy, hurling the opener in the sink and splashing dirty water over me. I carried on peeling spuds, not game to respond. I watched her catch sight of her flaming red hair in the oven door, grin at her reflection, then practise raising her eyebrows in startled expression, in case, as she told me, she ever got a job as an ABC newsreader.

Poppy's always held mixed feelings about her Scottish ancestry. She hates her hair and resents the inherited frugality which encourages her to do without. And she loathes her freckles. On the other hand she's thankful for thrift which encouraged her to invest the modest insurance money, culminating in the maturity of a pleasant but small nest egg.

You can't, I pointed out, have it both ways.

Poppy was two months shy of her fiftieth birthday, the boys financially independent, and the last of the family pets had flown to that great aviary in the sky when Poppy decided it was time to do something for herself. It was only fair and Robert, surely, would have been first to agree. I was second to agree as there's nothing I love more than spending other people's money. It's a special talent I have.

'Egypt!' announced Poppy. 'I'm going to Egypt.'

Robert had always wanted to see the pyramids of Gizeh. She would see them for him. No. Better than that, she would take him with her, or a photograph of him — the nice happy shot, the one where he's holding a salmon he caught in Tasmania. That would do. Yes, I agreed, that would do nicely, although I couldn't match her enthusiasm over old Cheops' thirteen-acre sandcastle, even if it is terribly famous.

Despite my constant good example Poppy is not proficient at self-indulgence so Robert's inclusion in proceedings gave her a comfortable justification for going. Nevertheless it was difficult for her not to be tempted by cheap fares and special hotel deals, and it was a very light-headed Poppy who emerged from the travel agents' with a business class return to Cairo, two weeks accommodation at a five star hotel, and a three day cruise on the Nile. Two weeks later I waved enthusiastically as Poppy flew to Cairo with a suitcase full of borrowed clothes and the photograph of Robert tucked safely in her handbag.

She sent me a postcard of the Great Pyramid:

> Egypt incredible.
> Hotel fabulous.
> Food delicious.
> Love Poppy.

Full of information, that's Poppy, although it did sound as if she and Robert were having a good time. I was glad for them.

Much later Poppy confided to me that she took Robert everywhere. At the Pyramids, when no one was looking, she withdrew Robert's photograph from her bag and showed him the sights. She talked to him too, told him about Gizeh and the latest diggings, and at night when Poppy reclined on her luxurious Egyptian cotton sheets Robert became the bookmark in *Death on the Nile*, the Agatha Christie I had given her.

Towards the end of the second week the hotel held a dinner dance and Poppy dressed up in the designer dress she'd tried on in an exclusive store in London, photographed herself wearing in the changing room, and gone home and copied.

Realising people would consider her odd if she danced with a picture of a man holding a salmon Poppy tucked Robert away in her book and went to dinner alone. After the meal a band replaced the violinist, lights dimmed, and red candles were placed on tables. Very romantic, Poppy supposed, for those so inclined. Not your sort of thing, Maggie, she'd said, which upset me because dark smoky rooms full of eastern promise are definitely my sort of thing. I'd have made a very good Turkish Delight girl.

Poppy sat quietly and sipped her brandy, trying to suppress a nagging guilt over deserting Robert. She watched amorous couples oil elegantly around the dance floor, and to take her mind off Robert she tried to guess where people were from and what they did for a living.

In her sweeping surveillance of the room Poppy caught sight of a singularly handsome man sitting alone on the other side of the floor. Her heart skipped a beat when she realised he had noticed her too. For almost half an hour they played a sort of staring/glance away/ I'm not really looking at you game. Flirting at fifty paces, Poppy called it.

Poppy was unsure of his age but he looked in his mid-forties. It was difficult to tell in the lighting, especially with the smoke, and she wasn't going to put her prescription glasses on. It was too late anyway as he'd stood up and was walking towards her. He was smiling and Poppy smiled back. Well, she thought, it wouldn't hurt to have a drink with him.

When he was ten feet away his smile changed to a look of panic. Poppy noticed with alarm he was all of twenty-five. What the hell would he do? He'd come too far to turn round. Poppy was crestfallen, and felt all fifty of her advancing years. She took a large swig of brandy.

'I'm sorry,' he said nervously, 'but from across the room I thought you were — um — I thought — well, I thought you were my mother.'

Initial fury gave way to embarrassment, and somewhere in the back of Poppy's mind stirred memories of a vaudeville entertainer recounting a not dissimilar scenario — one of those funny men she and Robert had seen at the Winter Gardens in Bournemouth on their honeymoon. Suddenly she remembered the punch line and recalled how Robert had laughed. Filled with newfound confidence, Poppy sneered at the young man and waggled her wedding ring in his face.

'I can't possibly be your mother, sonny Jim,' she said tartly, 'I'm married!'

Robert would have been so proud.

So very proud.

Poppy couldn't wait to tell him.

A postscript to this story. Poppy recently married a widowed engineer with three grown-up daughters. As I write, Poppy is making the first of what I imagine will be a succession of wedding dresses ...

Red Cabbage with Tasmanian Blue Cheese Dressing

This is a novel and delicious way to serve a red cabbage that, I'm sure, you plucked from the kitchen garden before supper.

You will need:

½ red cabbage
1 bottle blue cheese dressing (this creamy European-style dressing should be in your supermarket fridge. I made up the Tasmanian part)

Method: Remove rough outside leaves, thinly slice cabbage and place in a large bowl. Pour over enough blue cheese dressing to give a 'coleslaw' consistency. Toss well.

Presentation: Transfer to an attractive salad bowl, and to prove your talents aren't confined by tradition, serve at the end of the meal. Yes, it cleanses the palette after dessert, and leaves guests with a lasting impression of your innovative catering. It also means that, with a bit of luck, they won't break wind until they get home.

Salad Kebabs

The colourful elegance of these flamboyant kebabs will add real gaiety to your table. The quantities of fruit will vary depending on how many you are making.
  You will need:

Cherry tomatoes
Chilled fresh pineapple (I buy peeled and cored fresh pineapple
in sealed bags at the supermarket)
Firm ripe avocadoes, skin removed
Wooden kebab sticks
Baby spinach leaves (sold ready washed in
packets at the supermarket)
1 bottle honey and mustard salad dressing (or your
favoured sweet dressing)
Fresh coriander

Method: Wash, dry, and halve tomatoes. Cut pineapple and avocado into suitable sized pieces. Carefully thread tomato, pineapple, and avocado onto kebab sticks. Avoid putting avocado on the ends as it drops off!
Presentation: Scatter baby spinach leaves onto a large platter and place kebabs on top. Drizzle dressing over kebabs, sprinkle with chopped fresh coriander and serve immediately.

Tom Tom Tabouleh

Alias tomatoes filled with cracked wheat and things green. This exotic 'Middle-East meets Channel Islands' recipe is so easy that if you stuff it up, I think you should return to your village in disgrace.
  You will need:

Equal-sized ripe tomatoes that stand upright
A tub of fresh tabouleh from the supermarket or deli
Coarsely grated lemon rind

Method: Wash and dry tomatoes. Slice off top, about 2cm down, and scoop out insides. Generously fill tomatoes with tabouleh.
Presentation: If tomatoes refuse to stand at attention, level off bottoms with a knife. Don't be tempted to decorate with more parsley. Top instead with coarsely grated lemon rind.

Thai Beef Salad

I have yet to meet anyone who does not consume this with a passion. It is utterly scrumptious, incredibly easy and very impressive. You can omit the chilli if you wish.
You will need:

500g lean grilling steak (porterhouse, New York cut,
eye fillet, or rib)
1 red onion, chopped
1 punnet cherry tomatoes, halved
1 red pepper, sliced
1 Lebanese cucumber, sliced
1 bottle Thai salad dressing
1 red chilli, finely sliced
Fresh coriander, chopped

Method: Heat grill until very hot. Grill steaks on each side for a few minutes only — do not overcook! Allow meat to stand for ten minutes, then slice thinly. Combine steak with red onion, tomatoes, red pepper and cucumber. Pour on Thai salad dressing to taste. Toss well.
Presentation: Transfer salad to a flat platter and garnish with chilli and coriander.

Curried Coleslaw

I hope by now you have discovered the bags of ready-diced dry slaw ingredients in your supermarket vegetable department. I have added a couple of extra ingredients to vary the taste and texture, and I'm sure you'll agree the result is a treat for the taste buds.

You will need:

1 bag dry slaw
½ cup unsalted peanuts
½ cup sultanas
1 bottle coleslaw dressing (occasionally I use ranch dressing)
Curry powder (1 teaspoon curry powder for each ½ cup dressing used)

Method: Combine dry slaw, peanuts and sultanas. Measure required amount of dressing to suit personal taste, and add curry powder as indicated. Chill well.

Presentation: I usually transfer this to another dish with clean sides. There is no need for artistic frippery on top. This easy and delicious salad will stand alone!

Cauliflower Salad with Sweet Chilli and Ginger

The best thing about cauliflower is its crunchability. I have yet to be presented with an appetising method of cooking this exceedingly pretty vegetable, and I suspect lack of colour has a great deal to do with it being rather a bland and unexciting pile on a plate. Fear no more. I have the solution! Cauliflower should be eaten raw to retain the aforementioned crunchability, and served with a brilliantly coloured sauce for dipping. This combination is absolutely delicious.

You will need:

1 beautiful pure white cauliflower
1 bottle sweet chilli sauce with ginger
(a Thai sauce — there are several brands on the shelves)

Method: Rinse cauliflower under running water and cut into bite-sized florets, leaving a small stem for holding. Transfer sweet chilli and ginger sauce into a bowl and hide the bottle.
Presentation: Arrange the florets in an attractive bowl and serve with your superb sauce. It is important that you make appropriate comments at the table, such as 'Have I put enough chilli in?'

N.B. I often have this for lunch with a very cold glass of white burgundy. A marvellous way to start the afternoon.

Letterbox Update

High drama. The person who used my pastry brush to paint round the light switches has moved the bricks earmarked for our new letterbox. The bricks are now at the bottom of our garden, piled suspiciously in a 'BBQ' formation. I do not believe the metal plate is a base for the letterbox. I do not believe the logs are for the roof. I do not believe the tongs are to retrieve letters from the back corner. I do not believe 'How to build a better barbeque' is a school home reader.

Chapter Nine

Sandwiches

*'Hey chaps, stop what you're doing and come
and look at this.'*

— JOHN MONTAGU, FOURTH EARL OF SANDWICH,
A KITCHEN SOMEWHERE IN ENGLAND, 1762

I know it's hard to believe, but I am actually a trained sandwich person. At the tender age of sixteen I was let loose on the production line at a Gosport bakery. Madge the manageress, wary of my adolescent ability, started me on rolls. I was responsible for slicing a tomato, making a second cut in the top of a cheese roll, and tucking a tomato slice into the cut. This segregation stopped the cheese going soggy from the tomato juices. I did well, progressed to sandwiches, and was presented with a team outfit.

At this point in my life I was five foot seven and thin as a post. My white gaberdine cotton zip-up-the-front uniform had previously belonged to Daphne Unsworth, spinster of this parish, and no amount of washing could rid it of the aroma of lavender eau de cologne. Perhaps I should mention that Daphne never married because she was eighteen foot tall and sixteen foot wide. And stank of lavender.

To complete the outfit a large white paper surgeon's cap was secured over my Sybil's Home Salon haircut. I looked like a worker in a Russian nuclear power plant, but I didn't care. My mother kept telling me beauty fades but dumb is forever, so I held my head high, filled those sandwiches and carried on scaring the customers.

Sandwich Tips

- A correctly filled sandwich can be as nutritious as a cooked meal.
- Fillings fall out of sandwiches that are not buttered (except the ones in this chapter, of course).
- Real butter is the key to sandwich taste, but it's hard to spread. My Nana overcame this by dipping a knife in boiling water, swiping it on butter a few times, then spreading the 'melted' butter onto the cut end of a whole loaf. Once buttered, she would cut off the slice. Worked every time.
- Hang onto that old butter dish. Butter will make a huge comeback, and it's difficult to buy a butter dish anywhere at the moment.

The Recipes

I have been feeding Rudy the labrador (our neighbourhood sandwich expert) with properly aged sandwiches for six years. At 4p.m. each afternoon I remove said sandwiches from a school lunchbox and hurl them over the fence. It's an eagerly anticipated daily routine and Rudy, bless his golden socks, believes I make the best sandwiches in the Southern Hemisphere.

Rudy's owner, Nina, begs to differ. Nina says she makes the best sandwiches in the Southern Hemisphere, and to prove it sent me this startlingly scrumptious offering. I agree with Nina. Rudy is wrong. He ain't nothin' but a hound dog …

Nina's Elvis Sandwich

I'm sure there is no need to inform you too many of these may cause you to break into song and dress in diamante jumpsuits. It is, however, truly delicious.

You will need:

1 electric sandwich maker
Thick sliced bread from the bakery
Butter
½ over-ripe banana, mashed
1 tablespoon good quality smooth peanut butter

Method: Butter the outside of two bread slices and place, butter side down, on a bread board. Spread one slice with mashed banana and the other with peanut butter. Bring slices together, butter side out. Heat sandwich maker and cook sandwich until bread is toasted golden brown.

Presentation: Serve immediately. Woof woof!

I should also tell you Nina invented 'love sandwiches' and 'hate sandwiches'. Her 'love sandwich' is simple. Right between the filling and bread is an invisible layer of love. A 'hate sandwich' is more complex. Right between the filling and bread is a perfectly trimmed sheet of paper declaring 'YOU ARE AN ARSEHOLE'. Nina assures me it's the ultimate last word, perfect in a husband's lunchbox.

Nina's Story

In addition to Nina's obvious capabilities for making sandwiches, she also has some crafty picnic tricks. Nina told me one of the first things she learned after moving to the Gold Coast was how to smuggle homemade sandwiches past the 'NO FOOD TO BE TAKEN ON THESE PREMISES' sign at local theme parks — not exactly the crime of the century, more the cutting edge of budgetary anxiety over paying fifteen dollars for lunch and a drink.

This sin against corporate Australia added another dimension to Nina's day when she visited a park. The anticipation of getting caught was quite thrilling — a reminiscence of the time in childhood when you tear off the cloth label under the sofa that declares 'It is an offence to remove this label'. You wait ages for someone to arrest you, but no one ever does.

Nina says it's a good idea to have a story ready in case sandwich security officers, known as the SS, approach you. Her particular favourite is, 'My family suffers from a rare alimentary disorder which requires us to eat an enormous lunch purchased from Woolworths at Burleigh Heads, and I have a letter from my doctor if you wish to see it'. In the face of such Machiavellian brilliance it's a shame she's never been asked to produce it.

Over the years Nina has perfected her game plan. She parks near the entrance, and at lunchtime nips out and makes elaborate salad-packed sandwiches on the front seat of the car and smuggles them back through the entrance in a towel.

This system worked a dream until a hot day at, of all places, Dreamworld. Nina reports the family spent the morning on rides, and then took a dip in the pool to cool off before lunch. While other family members dried and dressed, Nina had her hand stamped and went out to the car and prepared sumptuous salad sandwiches, returned to the park with her hidden booty, and the family adjourned to the open-air restaurant to eat. The epitome of cheek.

From their table they could see there was no queue for the roller coaster, so Nina's husband nipped off with the elder children to have a ride before eating, a wise and unusual initiative, I must add, for a man who has parted his hair on the wrong side for thirty years.

Nina settled her infant daughter in the stroller on the far side of the table, and handed her a salad sandwich. Then Nina sat down, still in damp swimmers, and glowed with pride as passing parents nodded their approval at her beautiful child eating sensible food. Wholemeal too! What a good, caring, thoughtful mother she was. Maybe a passer-by would nominate her for Mother of the Year. Maybe the food editor of a major magazine would appear and beg Nina to write a column on children's dietary requirements. Maybe her daughter would eat the sandwich!

Then the sun went behind a cloud and Nina shivered. She is very hygiene aware, and did not wish to take eating offspring to the ladies while she changed, so Nina draped a towel over herself and discreetly undressed at the table. Not a difficult task, you'd imagine, for a veteran of the English seashore who could change behind a Marks and Sparks face washer.

It was an artfully tricky business divesting herself of the wet swimmers, but after some ferocious tugging Nina succeeded in reaching total nudity behind the towel. She smiled sweetly at other people in the restaurant and hoped they thought she was huddling against the sudden chill.

Nina adjusted the towel, and was just hunkering down behind the table, attempting to put on knickers, when two enormous ibis, smelly scavenging birds with long dangerous beaks, decided they would like a bite of her daughter's sandwich. They jumped on the stroller and took several aggressive pecks at the child's lunch.

'No!' Nina screeched sharply, and the ibis flapped their wings and launched into full ornithological warfare. Nina's daughter, quite rightfully, applied the bellows.

Nina couldn't move from her contorted position on the other

side of the table without causing serious embarrassment to herself, or major distress to the dining public. She remained frozen to the spot, and, with her head showing just above the table and her naked body hidden beneath it, she grinned broadly at everyone while her child broke the sound barrier.

'Give the nice birdies the sandwich darling,' said Nina through clenched teeth. The smile was practically all the way round her head.

The child couldn't hear her. She was in full throttle. Arms and feet and feathers and claws were flying everywhere.

'Give the birdie wirdies the sandwich darling,' Nina shouted gaily, 'birdies want the sandwich,' but she had only to look at the determination on her child's face to realise there was no way any birdie wirdie was getting that sandwich. After all, there's Viking blood in that child.

By this time people were staring and tut-tutting and wondering who to report Nina to, so she smiled her life-is-beautiful smile, the one reserved for special occasions, and watched as her daughter and the birds fought to the death. Nina was Roman centurion, Baldus Buttus. Bring out the Christians! Release the lions!

Nina smiled and smiled. She smiled at shocked Japanese tourists. She smiled at horrified park attendants. She smiled at her enraged daughter. She was just one big bodiless smile.

Then her daughter hit one of the sacred birds of Africa over the head with an ergonomic drink bottle. Both birds screeched in alarm, jumped off the stroller, and flapped around in circles, their campaign foiled. Nina started to laugh. Uncontrollably. The word hysteria springs to mind. I tell you, Hitchcock's got nothing on Nina when it comes to upsetting the general public, and as a demonstration of the power of nature she'd shot the mother defending her cubs theory right out the window — all the way to the moon.

Through streaming eyes Nina saw stunned disapproval on the audience's faces. Obviously they'd never seen an environmentally correct nature show before. Nina's daughter, red-faced from battle, gave a loud sigh and resumed lunch. She waved to the ibis as they staggered off to another table. 'How easy the young forgive,' Nina mused, as she quickly finished dressing.

Shortly, the rest of the family returned from their ride on the roller coaster. The children were flushed with excitement, but Nina's husband was as white as a sheet. He threw his cap on the table, shook his head and said, 'That ride was horrendous. You have no idea what I've just been through Nina, no idea at all.'

And if I might say so, this is typical of a man.

Natural Tahini and Honey Sandwiches

Tahini, apart from being a pretty word, is a delicious paste made from sesame seeds. Its distinctive flavour combines well with either honey or peanut butter to form a nutritious filling — don't tell children it's good for them, and they'll eat it by the truckload — that sort of deal.

You will need:

Honey
Tahini (usually in a jar in the health food section
of your supermarket)
1 sliced white loaf from the bakery

Method: Mix together equal parts of honey and tahini, and spread mixture between two slices of bread. There is no need for butter, but if you must, you must.
Presentation: These sandwiches work well in lunchboxes, or, cut daintily 'like what you was taught', for a work morning tea.

Toasted Chicken Sandwiches
with Brie and Cranberry

This is a pleasant, light meal for those times when you can't bear to put the stove on and no one's really hungry. It fills the spot nicely.

You will need:

> 1 electric sandwich maker
> Butter
> Thick sliced bread from the bakery
> Cooked chicken
> Ripe brie
> Snow pea sprouts, trimmed
> A jar of cranberry jelly

Method: Butter, and I mean 'butter', the outsides of two bread slices and place them butter-side down on the bread board. Next place some chicken on one piece of bread and top with thin slices of brie, snow pea sprouts, and a dollop of cranberry jelly. Top with the other slice of bread, butter side up. Heat sandwich maker and gently place sandwich onto grill plate. Cook until bread is nicely toasted.
Presentation: Slice sandwiches diagonally and place on a dinner plate with a sprig of basil or coriander.

Mrs Hopkins' Ultimate Garden Party Sandwich

I imagine, like me, you're constantly searching for a new and exciting sandwich to serve at your next garden party. I discovered this exquisite combination in the boot of Mrs Hopkins' car in the car park at the 1978 Melbourne Cup. Positively drips class, me dear. Like Mrs H, actually.

You will need:

> Ripe strawberries
> Cream cheese (at room temperature)
> 1 sliced white loaf from the bakery

Method: Wash and hull strawberries, and slice very thinly. Spread a thin layer of cream cheese to edges of two slices of bread. Place strawberry slices in a single layer over one slice, then top with second slice of bread, cream cheese side down. Remove crusts and cut diagonally.
Presentation: Eat. Make another one. Eat. Make another one. Eat. Make another one. Eat ...

Salad Bagelwich with Hummus and Baby Spinach

Philosophers have agonised over bagels for hundreds of years. Me, I've been at it for two. Is the hole the essence of a bagel? Are bagels supposed to give you indigestion? Whatever the answers, bagels are high fashion food and therefore a must for your Hoax Cuisine portfolio.

You will need:

Fresh bagels
A tub of hummus (a chick pea dip from the supermarket)
Red onion, finely sliced
Baby spinach leaves (or rocket leaves)
Continental cucumber, finely sliced

Method: Slice bagel in half and spread some hummus on lower half. Top with red onion, baby spinach leaves, and cucumber.
Presentation: Serve on a plate with a few baby spinach or rocket leaves.

The BLT

A bacon, lettuce and tomato sandwich is, without doubt, America's finest national sanger. There is nothing on earth as intoxicating as the marriage of sweet juicy tomatoes, the salty tang of bacon, and cool crisp garden lettuce.

You will need:

Thick sliced bread
Short cut bacon, fat removed
Ripe tomato, sliced crossways
Good quality mayonnaise
Crisp lettuce leaves (I use cos lettuce)

Method: Toast bread. Grill bacon until crispy. On one piece of toast put a layer of tomato slices and cover with crispy bacon. Squirt on a healthy dollop of good quality mayonnaise and top with lettuce and finally sandwich lid.
Presentation: Slice sandwich diagonally and serve with a glass of Coca Cola and a baseball game on the TV.

Picnic Loaf with Summer Vegetable Filling

Quite honestly, this is the easiest and tastiest way to make one enormous sandwich for a picnic. There are no set quantities and you can vary the guts of it to suit what's in your fridge.
   You will need:

1 fresh French loaf (baguette)
1 ripe avocado, mashed with a squirt of lemon juice
¼ red onion, finely chopped
Sliced tomato
Sliced red pepper
Sliced cucumber
Snow pea sprouts, trimmed
Good quality mayonnaise

Method: Slice loaf lengthways but don't cut right through. Spread avocado over lower half, and fill with all other vegetables. Finally spread a thin layer of mayonnaise on inside of lid. Press together lightly, and tuck in stragglers.
Presentation: Wrap in foil or slip back into the baguette bag until required. Slice big healthy portions at picnic time and grind fresh pepper onto the grown-ups' servings.

Letterbox Update

I had a dream ...

... the council used Crusty for one of the speed bumps at the new shopping centre. I drove my trusty steed at that sucker full speed. Again and again. A crowd gathered. Over the sound of triumphant cheering I heard nervous commentary: 'There are many sets of eyes glued to these two ... cuts it very close there ... tackled that one well ... a true mark of class ...'

I made a final approach. Whack. Thud. Bump. Applause.

'Oh well done,' sang the commentator, 'she'll be well pleased with that one, well pleased ...'

Chapter Ten

Snacks

*If the snack you're eating between meals isn't ruining
your appetite, then you haven't eaten enough yet!*

I know this to be true. I'm big on snacks between meals, so it's
lucky I had an active upbringing and avoided laying down fat cells
in childhood. I saved that for later.

Mum wouldn't be impressed with my modern image. Not at all,
at all. She believed, like most of her generation, that snacks were
unhealthy and obesity the result of laziness. I seem to recall there
wasn't a single teenage weight problem that couldn't be cured by
team sport, early rising, three square meals a day and whizzing a
vacuum cleaner round one's bedroom.

Imagine my defiant teenage joy when a nurse tutor at Kings
College Hospital informed our class snacks could be healthy, and
many weight problems were caused by glandular disease. What
magnificent argument ammunition. Naturally I jumped the next
train home to tell Mum the nurse tutor's good news.

'Sucks boo to that,' she snapped, and commenced a half-hour
dissertation on the war, washing, weeding, walking forty miles a
day, taking out the garbage and riding my bicycle back to London.
'Go tell that to Nurse Tutu!' she exclaimed.

Snack Tips

- A proper snack provides maximum benefit from minimum preparation.
- It is not written in stone that snacks have to be healthy. Bring on the ice cream sandwiches I say.
- And a tip for those of you on a diet — snack *instead* of meals, not in addition to!

The Recipes

There are three kinds of snacks: those you have when people are looking, those you have when they aren't, and lastly, those you have when you've drunk too much on an empty stomach. Our guest recipe owes its origin to the latter.

One afternoon, after duteous housework and parenting aplenty, my neighbour Suzy and I got stuck into the Blackberry Nip she had left over from a home wine-tasting. We sure showed that bottle who was boss, and faced with urgent sobering requirements raided the fridge, only to find leftover fruit loaf and Roaring Forties cheese (a delicious Tasmanian blue cheese, as heavenly as Stilton). Needs must, and we devoured the lot.

This is how Suzy and I discovered the snack of the century, the most mouth-wateringly delectable combination possible. In fact it was so good we opened a Spatlese to help it down. Neither of us remembers who first claimed ownership of the recipe, so we compromised. Suzy owns the recipe — as long as she never invites me to a wine-tasting party.

Suzy's Fruit Loaf with Roaring Forties Cheese

You will need:

1 unsliced fruit loaf (retains the possibility you made it yourself
— don't forget to discard packaging)
Roaring Forties cheese

Method: Cut a few dainty slices from the fruit loaf. Ensure Roaring Forties is at room temperature, and peel off top layer of blue wax, exposing cheese.
Presentation: Place fruit loaf slices and Roaring Forties cheese on a bread board. Spread a little cheese on some fruit loaf, so over-proof guests get the idea. A few frozen grapes wouldn't go astray either (to freeze grapes simply put them in a plastic bag in freezer).

I told you it was the snack of the century. Be warned, once tried there is no going back. Suzy even has it for breakfast. She says it's sophisticated and makes up for wearing fuzzy Kmart slippers.

Suzy's Story

Suzy's also a very aural person, which explains why she likes her front room full of chattering wine tasters. Under laboratory conditions her favourite sound is 'room service', but she also enjoys the marine acoustics of chugging ferries and clanking yacht masts, two sensory pleasures that, during early motherhood years, saw her a frequent visitor to Cremorne Point in Sydney Harbour. There's a wooden seat on the eastern side of the point that is a perfect spot to feast on these auditory delights. You can't go there, because it's Suzy's seat. I'm just telling you about it, okay.

In those faraway days, when the world had gone to work, Suzy and her daughter would laze in bed and read *Spot*, play a little peepo, then stroll down to the western side of Cremorne Point for a swim. Afterwards they took a leisurely nap on the warm grass, drying in the sun, before ambling round the headland to Suzy's seat.

Immediately below the seat is a stone birdbath with little

concrete animals cemented around the base. Suzy's daughter liked to wash the animals with water from the birdbath, and as they dried quickly in the heat this domestic chore took a considerable amount of time. There was nothing for Suzy to do but replenish the birdbath as required, and sit back and listen to the occasional woody thud of a ferry hitting Old Cremorne Wharf, and the long eerie creak of settling timber which echoed round the bay as yacht masts danced noisy jigs in the wake.

After a picnic lunch they'd climb down to the water's edge and look for fish and throw skimming stones, and frequently one of them would fall in. Some days they'd play hide and seek and get mosquito bites and itch like crazy. Other times they'd lie on rocks, munch apples, and watch the clouds go by. But mostly they washed concrete animals and sat and listened. It was a demanding routine and I can certainly see why Suzy drinks.

One day, at Cremorne Point, a smartly dressed woman sat down beside Suzy on her seat. Suzy told her there were red-back spiders around, but the woman just smiled and said, 'It's lovely here, isn't it?'

'Yes,' replied Suzy.

'Is that your little girl?' she asked.

'Yes.'

'What a lovely outfit,' she said, admiring the old curtain Suzy'd turned into a child's pinafore dress. 'Did you make it?'

'Yes,' said Suzy.

They sat silently for a while, watching the concrete platypus get a good soaking.

'You could sell those dresses to shops,' remarked the woman (and to be fair, I have to interject here and tell you it was a very pretty dress).

'I'm not that good at sewing,' responded Suzy, 'it's a one-off.'

'You wouldn't have to make them,' said the woman, 'you could pay other people to run them up for you. You could concentrate on the marketing.'

They resumed silence. Suzy's daughter slipped over and had to be kissed on a sore knee. Then Suzy had to kiss the turtle and the rabbit because they had sore knees too. The 2 o'clock ferry chugged past. Suzy nearly missed it.

'It's very demanding being a mother, isn't it?' said the woman.

'Yes,' Suzy agreed, thinking there were few jobs that required you to perform intimate random acts of kindness on garden ornaments.

'Don't you get bored? I mean, don't you crave a bit more excitement?'

'We do jigsaws,' answered Suzy, and smiled lest the woman think her rude.

'Don't you miss adult company?'

'I watch television,' said Suzy, still smiling.

'You know,' the woman said again, 'you could start a small business selling those dresses.'

'It's a thought,' said Suzy, vaguely intrigued. The accidental couturist!

'You could control the product manufacture and distribution,' the woman explained, 'and you could employ a marketing firm to help you.'

Suzy thought her companion was getting a bit ahead of herself, but let her waffle on about tax benefits and the small business advisory service while she herself helped a junior board member pee in the bushes.

'Would it take long to set up?' Suzy asked, returning to her seat and making idle conversation.

'No, a small enterprise like that could be up and running in no time.'

'I wouldn't have the time,' muttered Suzy, nodding towards her daughter.

'You have to make time,' the woman said forcefully. 'I did a degree in commerce when my children were little. It's amazing what you can do if you try.'

A blue-winged kookaburra flew onto a nearby limb, shortly joined by another, and the pair of them chortled away until a territorial magpie shot through the trees on a bombing raid. Suzy's daughter clapped her hands in delight. 'Naughty maggie,' she sang, and grinned cheekily. 'Naughty maggie ... naughty maggie ... naughty maggie ...'

'I really don't think I'm cut out for the business world,' admitted Suzy, thrilling at her daughter's delight.

'Sure you are,' the woman replied, 'anyone can do it. Anyway, it would be better than wasting your time washing nappies. You'd be able to pay someone else to do that for you.'

'Doesn't it take years to make profits in a new business?' asked Suzy.

'Oh,' she said, 'in about three or four years you should be making money. The secret to a successful business is planning. There are courses you can take.'

'I wouldn't have time,' said Suzy, realising this woman must think her most disorganised, 'I'm very busy at home. It's never-ending you know. Accounts and things.' Yeah, right, like Suzy spends her evenings adding up.

The woman grinned at Suzy and announced, 'In a few years' time, if it's well established, you could branch into mail order. There's big money to be made in mail order.'

'Really,' Suzy said, wanting the woman to go away so she could have a cup of Darjeeling tea from her crummy old thermos. Suzy has standards.

'Yes,' the woman continued, 'and a few years after that you could sell the business and sit back on your laurels. You'd be able to do whatever you wanted. You could read books, go for walks, sit in the sun, play with your children ... oh my goodness, is that the time ... I have to go ... I've an important meeting.'

'Me too,' Suzy said, anxiously looking at her watch.

But she didn't mention it was with the 2.30 ferry.

Did you spot the moral in this story? That's right. Always throw out your old curtains.

Nifty Nachos

This is a larruping good snack that can be shared by several people from the same plate. From the same planet too!

You will need:

1 packet corn or tortilla chips
1 x 440g can kidney beans
½ cup good quality spaghetti sauce
¼ cup sour cream
2 cups grated cheddar cheese

Method: Scatter corn chips in an ovenproof dish. Mix together kidney beans, spaghetti sauce and sour cream, and spoon over corn chips. Sprinkle on cheddar cheese. Bake at 180°C for about 15 minutes.

Presentation: This snack is best eaten with fingers, so serve with a large pile of paper serviettes.

Smoked Australian Salmon with Capers

Quate nace with pre-dinner drinks, this tantalising union replaces nibbles and entrée, effectively killing two birds with one stone.

You will need:

1 French loaf (baguette)
Cream cheese
1 packet smoked salmon
1 red onion, peeled and sliced into fine rings
1 bottle capers
1 lemon cut into wedges

Method: Cut French loaf diagonally into healthy slices. Spread each slice with cream cheese. Place a thin layer of smoked salmon over cheese, and top with some red onion rings and a few capers.

Presentation: Arrange on a platter and serve with lots of lemon wedges. Lemon should be squeezed on salmon just before eating.

Pumpernickel Bread with Emmenthal and Apples

Here is another Rolls Royce snack that, as the French would say, is worthy of a detour. Something exciting happens to human taste-buds when Emmenthal cheese and apple are popped into the mouth at the same time. It doesn't have the same effect eaten one after the other. I've tried it all ways (the things I've done for you).

You will need:

Emmenthal cheese
Juicy apples
Sliced pumpernickel bread

Method: Extremely difficult preparation here. Place a slice of Emmenthal and a slice of apple on a slice of pumpernickel bread. Of course if you dislike pumpernickel (and I have to admit I'm crazy about the word), use biscottes or nothing, but it's not as good as with pumpernickel, pumpernickel, pumpernickel.

Presentation: This is a very grown-up snack so don't expect small folk to enjoy it. Big folk, however, will consume this delicious combination with gusto and gutso. Slice apples just before serving to avoid discolouration, and if you're feeling extra cosmopolitan insert a glass of well-chilled white burgundy into the menu.

Ice Cream Sandwiches

Oh yes, I was deadly serious about ice cream sandwiches. I'm fed up with reading about healthy snacks that involve raw carrots in heavy disguise. Ice cream sandwiches are good fun to make and even better to eat.

You will need:

> 1 packet milk arrowroot biscuits
> 1 jar strawberry conserve
> Strawberry ice cream (slightly softened)

Method: To prevent biscuits from snapping, prepare sandwiches on a clean folded tea towel. Spread one biscuit with a thin layer of strawberry conserve, and the other with 1cm thick layer of strawberry ice cream. Bring biscuits together and press lightly. Place in the freezer for ten minutes before eating.
Presentation: No hanging about, folks. Consume immediately.

Samosas with Sweet Lemon Myrtle Chilli Sauce

It's considered frightfully 'in' to serve Australian bush foods, and this combination of traditional Indian and native Oz is hard to top. If you can't find Sweet Lemon Myrtle Chilli Sauce, substitute with a good quality sweet chilli sauce.
    You will need:

> 1 packet frozen samosas (several good brands out there,
> and my preference is for lentil and vegetable samosas)
> 1 bottle Sweet Lemon Myrtle Chilli Sauce

Method: Preheat oven to 180°C. Place frozen samosas on a foil-lined baking tray and bake as per packet instructions, usually for eight to twelve minutes. Allow samosas to stand for five minutes before serving.
Presentation: Serve with a bowl of Sweet Lemon Myrtle Chilli sauce for dipping. I'm sorry, but you cannot pretend you made this sauce yourself. By all means go for the samosas, but the sauce is definitely advanced Hoax Cuisine only.

Mediterranean Dolmades with Tzatziki
and Lemon Garlic Olives

'Dolmades' is the name of those suspicious green parcels loitering in trays at the deli counter. They are edible vine leaves stuffed with rice, and wonderful served cold as a snack or appetizer. Dolmades are ready to eat when purchased; always a plus as you know!

Tzatziki is a dip made from yoghurt, cucumber, and garlic, and available at most supermarkets.

Olives are olives are olives. Except the ones used here which an industrious little soul in a kitchen somewhere has marinaded for you in lemon and garlic.

You will need:

> Dolmades (canned or from the supermarket deli,
> where they are probably from a larger can!)
> A tub of tzatziki (usually with the dips)
> Lemon and garlic olives (marinating in tubs at the
> supermarket deli. If you can't find them use
> regular Kalamata olives)
> Pita bread (optional)

Method and Presentation: If I am alone I dip dolmades into the tzatziki tub and eat olives from the sophisticated plastic container supplied by the store. If there are spectators I arrange dolmades, olives, and pita bread on an antipasto plate and transfer the tzatziki to my own 'tzatziki' bowl. And eat like a lady.

Letterbox Update

Crusty has complained to Australia Post about our mail delivery arrangements. I am in receipt of a stern letter from the authorities (funny how that one got through). We must now make a decision as to whether we back down or obtain legal assistance to insist our mail is deposited in the receptacles provided, namely a blue plastic bag in a poinciana tree, or an elevated milk churn. There is a principle at stake here. We displayed the letter on our kitchen noticeboard for three days, inviting comments. A decision has been made. We are using the paperwork to light the inaugural Groff brick barbeque that resides, in all its nouveau splendour, at the bottom of our garden. As Bertolt Brecht once said, 'Grub first, then ethics'.

Chapter Eleven

Just Desserts

Never trust a thin cook!

— OLD ENGLISH PROVERB

Several years ago my husband the star shopper (as opposed to my husband the human machete when pruning the garden) managed to purchase an unbelievably cheap deal on a Club Med holiday in Noumea. I hadn't been on a proper holiday in ages, and was wildly excited about eating French food for two weeks.

Imagine my surprise when our plane was greeted at Noumea airport by a Sherman tank. Apparently the star shopper hadn't thought a small military coup worthy of mention.

The food at Club Med is legendary. Entrée and main were served at table, and desserts displayed buffet style in an adjoining room. Not a table. A whole room! Working on the assumption I was probably going to die anyway, I decided to live my last days to the full, and steadily worked that room for 14 days. Not a morsel of meat passed my lips. Nor a skerrick of vegetable. Just desserts!

Dessert Tips

- Well, there's a huge tip in that little tale, for a start.
- Dessert preparation should be done well ahead of time (and yes, most of it by somebody else).

- Don't serve ready-made frozen desserts. Everyone recognises them, and you can do much better than this.
- Invest in a good ice-cream scoop — one with anti-freeze in the spoon part.
- Unless you've been under a rock lately you'll be aware the in thing is to serve dessert on top of the sauce. Preferably on a plate the size of a satellite dish. It shall no doubt take ten years for sauce to return to its rightful drizzle position. Hoax Cuisine cooks scoff at modern ways. Hoax Cuisine cooks like it on top!
- The trick to a perfect fruit platter is a really, really cold plate!
- You must understand crème fraiche as it's a common dessert accompaniment lately. Crème fraiche is French cream and it has a different flavour and quality to Australian cream. French cream is matured, allowing lactic acids and natural ferments to thicken cream and impart a nutty flavour. To make crème fraiche mix 300mls of Australian cream with 1 tablespoon of buttermilk. Put in a jar, shake well, and leave to stand at room temperature for a day or so until it's thickened. Quite simply, crème fraiche is a pain in the arse, and Hoax Cuisine cooks don't waste time preparing it for desserts while King Island is still part of Australia.
- Pop a vanilla bean in a jar of caster sugar for a week. It gives sugar a delicious flavour.

The Recipes

I don't bother with desserts unless visitors arrive, in which case it's a safe bet to assume I'll be feeling no pain by pudding time. I've learned from experience this is definitely not the moment to start making crepes suzettes, so you'll find these delectable dessert recipes are either ridiculously simple, or can be made the day before.

Talking of crepes, my Russian friend Niska makes the best blintzes ever. They're a type of pancake made with cottage cheese and sour cream. As Niska's the subject of this chapter's story, I was hoping she could provide a shortcut blintz recipe.

Let me give you another tip. Never ask a Russian for a shortcut traditional recipe. They put Lenin in a glass case because he asked the party chef for a quick way to make borscht. Suffice it to say, you will not need ingredients for blintzes.

Niska's Boysenberry Baroque

I can't tell you how many wodkas it took me to coax this recipe from Niska. I was tempted to call it Bombed Russian. Actually this is quite a sophisticated dessert as long as you keep it small and use the best ingredients.

You will need:

Good quality vanilla ice cream
1 can boysenberries
Almond bread wafers (in packets at the supermarket)

Method: Place one scoop of ice cream in a small dessert bowl. Spoon some boysenberries and their juice over one side of the ice cream (don't swamp it), and pop a couple of almond wafers in the top.

Presentation: As you place this knockout Hoax Cuisine dessert on the table dispel any suspicion the fruit came from a can by announcing, 'These boysenberries were flown in from the Channel Islands'.

Thanks Niska, but next time we will demand blintzes. Actually, I've realised another perfect reason for involving Niska in a chapter entitled 'Just Desserts'. Her life is one big run-in with authority, and her conversation peppered with anecdotes of verbal retaliation. I think you'll like this story of one such occasion, and perhaps recognise someone you know very, very, well.

Niska's Story

It was a bad fur hat day. Niska leapt from bed happy as a lark, put the kettle on, opened the fridge door, and a full carton of milk fell out and swam over the floor. Bending down to clean up, her forehead connected with the protruding handle on the freezer, and two seconds later blood dripped daintily onto Niska's white towelling dressing gown. Off to the bathroom to fetch a sticking plaster and discover the loo had sprung a leak. And, surprise surprise, the plaster box was empty. No doubt there was a teddy somewhere with a serious injury.

Next time this happens I have told Niska she must go straight back to bed. Unfortunately for the world at large, and particularly Jim Snape at our local hardware store, on the second Monday of last February she kept going.

By 9 a.m. Niska was a seething mass of maternal frenzy looking for an object upon which to vent the Russian spleen. Her family, on full alert, had skedaddled, so she took to the leaking loo with pliers, a hammer, and the three-in-one washer repair kit. Big mistake.

I should explain. There has not been a lavatory system invented that Niska cannot fix with O-rings, tape, super-glue, old bandages or the proper repair kit. She is conversant with 500 ways to use bathroom sealant, a legacy of growing up in a house built in fifteen-something where bathrooms were so old they had museum listings. You never called a plumber when a water diviner and a roll of plumber's tape would do.

Niska was mildly surprised to see the washer around the overflow on her relatively modern convenience had worn. This shouldn't happen, as there is no friction at this point to cause wear and tear. Nevertheless the washer was worn.

Replacing all other washers and, using number 46 of her 500 ways to use bathroom sealant, Niska affected a good seal at the base of the overflow. Didn't work, did it? Still leaking, wasn't it? Spanner hit wall, didn't it?

Furious, she removed the part and took it to the hardware store, which is really a warehouse on the industrial estate. It's the size of a small planet — you could probably build an airport from the fixtures and fittings section. Men named Bert or Tony stride manfully around in armpit-stained shirts and steel-capped shoes shouting 'Load up, load up,' while forklifts cha-cha in aisles and testosterone drips from metal girders.

The parking lot was full of workmen's trucks, delivery vans and station wagons so Niska had to park way round the corner outside the saddlery and walk back in the rain without an umbrella. I feel, in her defence, this unfairly contributed to the ruination of Jim's day. Someone had to get it. Niska chose Jim.

Jim's first mistake was to smile. It was Niska's bad mood; it belonged to her, and no joker with a spirit level was going to end it before she said so.

His second mistake was verbal. 'Can I help you, love?' he said.

Niska bristled (it's a Russian thing), but bit her suffragist tongue. Lucky for Jim, Niska had skipped her two per cent riboflavin that morning. It always makes her extra lippy.

Niska produced the overflow pipe and offending washer. Jim put on spectacles and examined them. Jim had watched Antiques Today. Then he shook his head, cleared his throat, and slapped at the cigarette packet in his shirt pocket. They learn this at the Hardware Academy.

'It's about thirteen years old,' he muttered. 'Don't make these any more.'

'Thirteen isn't old,' said Niska, and regaled him for ten minutes on toilets she had known in the old country. I think he was secretly rather impressed. I know I was.

Jim smirked, unaware the Russian had breakfasted on warm blood. He examined the washer more closely. 'These don't wear out,' he said.

'This one has,' replied Niska.

'Nah,' he said, 'that's not your problem, love. It'll be one of the other washers.'

Niska swallowed hard, as they say in detective novels, and looked at the ground for a few seconds. Slowly she raised her head, and then stuffed tense hands in deep pockets for safekeeping. Jim's safekeeping.

'Would you,' she asked politely, 'have said that to me if I was a man?'

Niska looked Jim squarely in the face, every doughy inch of it. He had, she told me later, assumed the on-guard position.

'You need a plumber,' he said defensively.

'Would you,' Niska repeated a little louder, 'have said that to me if I was a man?'

People were looking. Niska loves an audience.

'WOULD YOU,' she shouted, 'HAVE SAID THAT TO ME IF I WAS A MAN?'

Jim had backed in to the timber and mouldings aisle. Niska followed and seized the overflow from his sweaty grasp.

'I shall *never* purchase goods in this shop again,' she said sternly. 'And I will ensure every woman for a hundred miles knows of the disdain and outright chauvinism with which they are regarded in this store. I shall bring you to your knees and not rest until females in this town are given due respect for their plumbing capabilities. I shall make sure this incident is in the school newsletter and I will report you to the discrimination board, and it is my fervent hope the ensuing court case makes a huge and messy hole in your termination payout from this job, because that is what will happen if I have anything to do with it. Trust me, Jim. That is what will happen.'

At least, that's what Niska told the steering wheel on the way home.

Yes, you're correct. Niska meant the anti-discrimination board. I made valiant attempts to clarify this language discrepancy but Niska did more bristling and said, 'What would Australians know about grammar? You cut down a tree, then you cut it up.' She has a point.

Melon Classique

The flavours of different types of melon meld beautifully, and there's nothing more refreshing after a fine summer meal or a lazy afternoon barbeque than a platter of freshly chilled melon. This is a great dish for your Hoax Cuisine image, even if it isn't Hoax Cuisine at all!

You will need:

Chilled ripe rockmelon (seeds removed)
Chilled ripe honeydew melon (seeds removed)
Chilled ripe seedless watermelon
Crushed ice
Fresh mint

Method: Make sure everything is chilled, especially the platter. Leaving skin on, cut melons into manageable slices. Arrange artistically onto a platter of crushed ice — it should look like a riot of colour has tumbled onto the platter, not a neat row of melon soldiers.

Presentation: Serve au naturel with a few sprigs of fresh mint for garnish. As Enrico Caruso once said, melon is a good fruit. You eat, you drink, you wash your face ...

Fruit Salad

This is the simplest and most impressive dessert to feed a lot of folk at short notice. It's perfect for barbeques, alfresco breakfasts or large families coming to dinner. The emphasis should be on good quality products. I'm totally spoiled as I live near Tropical Fruit World in northern New South Wales, and often get quite out of control with weird and wonderful fruity experimentation.

You will need:

2 x 850g cans top quality fruit salad in syrup (something with the word 'exotic' in usually does the trick)

A combination of any of the following fresh fruits in season: strawberries, grapes, peaches, lychees, mangoes, apples, rockmelon, kiwifruit, pineapple, bananas, pears or pawpaw. Personally I like a lot of a few, and I favour bright colours, so I tend to purchase large quantities of only three colourful fresh fruits in season.

Method: Open cans! Pour contents into a large glass bowl. Prepare fresh fruits and add to bowl. Remember, if using banana, add just before serving.

Presentation: Chill well and serve with lashings of King Island cream.

Mango Sorbet

Early 70s London boasted a fun restaurant in Battersea called the House at Pooh Corner. The set menu was a riot of innuendo and pun (Fowl Agnew being my favourite), and while a chef trained in café theatre stood at your table and explained in detail how each dish was prepared, a large British bulldog named Satchmo would sneak onto a spare chair beside you.

Satchmo was addicted to Mango Sorbet and would patiently wait to see which flavour sorbet was ordered. I can't begin to tell you the sneer if you chose strawberry! I expect (no, I'm certain) Satchmo is in doggy heaven, and if you're out there Satch, this one's for you.

You will need:

1 can mangoes in heavy syrup
1 teaspoon lemon juice

Method: Freeze can of mangoes overnight. Open can, run hot water over sides and drop frozen contents into a blender. Add lemon juice. Separate frozen fruit with a knife to save your blades, and blend until smooth.

Presentation: Serve immediately in dainty bowls. Less is more with this dish.

Traditional Pavlova with Summer Fruits

Yes, it had to be here somewhere, didn't it? The adulation received when you present this lovely dessert is quite out of proportion to the effort required to make it, which is why it's a must for your Hoax Cuisine portfolio. I often see people make the base and cheat on the topping with artificial whipped cream and canned fruit. Hoax Cuisine cooks don't do that. No, no, no. We cheat on the base and use the very best fresh ingredients for the top!

You will need:

1 cup thickened cream
1 good quality pavlova base (readily available from the
supermarket in several sizes)
1 punnet ripe strawberries, hulled
1 punnet blueberries
2 kiwifruit, sliced
Pulp of 2 large ripe passionfruit

N.B. If using a very large pavlova base, increase all quantities. I expect you worked that one out, didn't you?

Method: Whip cream until it forms firm peaks. Spread cream over pavlova base. Artistically arrange berries and kiwifruit over cream, and drizzle on passionfruit pulp.
Presentation: Check for fingerprints before serving. You can also make this using individual pavlova shells. Yet another thing you worked out!

Celestial Strawberries with Grand Marnier

This dessert, as the name implies, is simply divine.
You will need:

2 punnets fresh ripe strawberries
6 tablespoons Grand Marnier
2 tablespoons caster sugar
Double thick cream
Rolled chocolate wafers (these European
wafers are sold in most supermarkets. There
are several flavours. They resemble long
cigars or pipes and if you stick them in your
nostrils you can pretend to be a walrus.)

Method: Hull strawberries and marinate in Grand Marnier and
sugar for an hour.
Presentation: Serve strawberries with a healthy dollop of double
thick cream and yummy rolled wafers.

Fresh Figs with Creamed Orange Zest

A must for your Hoax Cuisine image, Fresh Figs with Creamed
Orange Zest would not be out of place on the menu in one of the
world's top restaurants. Especially as the world's top restaurants are
currently all trying to emulate home cooking. Odd, isn't it?
You will need:

125g cream cheese, softened
1 tablespoon icing sugar
Finely grated rind of ½ an orange (reserve a little for garnish)
Fresh figs
Washed fig leaves for garnish (this may require a brisk walk
round the neighbourhood gardens)

Method: Blend together cream cheese, icing sugar, and finely grated orange rind. Taste test and add more orange rind if you wish. Halve figs, leaving stalk on.
Presentation: Place two fig halves on a small dessert plate. Place a neat scoop of Creamed Orange Zest next to figs, and complete design with artistically placed fig leaves. I also serve Creamed Orange Zest with Pumpkin Pie (p. 135).

Letterbox Update

I have a postal gem from America. In case you don't know, American postmen collect outgoing post from domestic letter-boxes, as well as deliver it. If you have stamped mail to collect you raise the little American flag on your box, so they know to stop.

My husband's folks live in a small town in upstate New York where everyone knows all about everybody. Their postman, Dirk, has been collecting mail addressed to me for many years. About ten years back he started jotting comments on the envelopes — your parents look well — snow drifts today — that sort of thing. I would make notes back to him on the outside of my envelopes, thanking him for his thoughtfulness. It was almost 84 Charing Cross Road there for a while.

Imagine my horror when I learned Dirk had been thrown in the slammer for tampering with US mail. Apparently he had 127 bags of undelivered mail in his basement, obviously intended for those who wouldn't play the envelope game. At least, I like to think so.

I have enlarged the newspaper clipping, placed it in a plastic sleeve, and nailed it to the poinciana tree where Crusty can see it. I have highlighted the phrase 'sentenced to fifteen years in a state penitentiary for non-delivery of mail'.

Chapter Twelve

Cakes and Pastries

The first cake I made was a Victoria sponge in what was known as Miss Butcher's domestic science class. It took a whole term. Indeed, many girls were so concerned about the lengthy procedure they started making plans for their wedding cakes. To this day I have never made another Victoria sponge. I simply don't have time.

Tips About Cakes and Pastry

- Research quality cake shops near home and ascertain which 'gateau' can be personalised at home.
- Either have no cake forks, or two sets, as each time they're needed you will have more than one set of people at your table.
- Locate the nearest gourmet cheesecake shop, know opening hours, and learn their menu. Most will obligingly sell half a cheesecake, and trust me, there's no way you could make one this good for the price. Reasonable enough, in fact, to justify being popped in a taxi for emergency afternoon tea occasions.
- Make a quick teacake by decorating a fresh supermarket single layer sponge. Spread a layer of raspberry jam over sponge. Whip ½ a cup of thickened cream with ½ teaspoon of icing sugar until it forms peaks. Spread over jam. Top with fresh raspberries.

The Recipes

Hoax Cuisine cooks need a repertoire of fine cakes that appear difficult but are in fact extremely simple to prepare. My friend Astrid (see, Meredith, I told you I wouldn't use your real name) owns a cake shop in Victoria. It was a coffee lounge when she bought it, but Astrid's class act with flour and Charlotte Malakoff au Chocolat quickly transformed her shop into a gateau mecca.

As I suspected, the recipe for Charlotte Whatsit is not available for general consumption. Astrid wormed her way out of this by informing me that, 'your readers, my dear, need to know how to prepare Napoleons, as they are taking the restaurant world by storm'. Naturally Astrid knew the easy method of preparing these flamboyant individual cakes.

Astrid's Emperor Napoleons

Don't be deterred by the idea and instructions. It's incredibly easy. In simple terms you bake the pastry, prepare the fillings, then layer everything. This recipe makes nine Napoleons.

You will need:

3 sheets puff pastry, thawed
1 cup thickened cream
2 teaspoons icing sugar
1 teaspoon vanilla essence
1 jar lemon butter (also known as lemon curd)
Icing sugar (for serving)

Method: Thaw pastry and cut each sheet into nine squares (about 8cm x 8cm each). Place all 27 squares on lightly greased baking trays and bake in a hot oven (220°C) for eight to ten minutes, or until puffed and golden brown. Remove from trays and cool on a wire rack. Meanwhile, whip cream with two teaspoons of icing sugar and vanilla essence until stiff peaks form.

As soon as the pastry has cooled you are ready to start building the Napoleons. The only tricky part is spreading the lemon butter without breaking the pastry — either spoon it on in small dollops, or use a piping bag if you're clumsy. Proceed as follows from base up: pastry square, a modest layer of lemon butter, pastry square, layer of cream, pastry square. Finally dust your Napoleons with sifted icing sugar.

Presentation: Congratulations. You have just bought yourself a night with Napoleon!

Astrid's Story

As I expected, Astrid tried to reorganise my book with wedding cakes, Christmas cakes, and her famous divorce cake. Just loves anything to do with an occasion, does our Astrid, which is probably why I asked her if she would like to come to Phillip

Island with me and share the wondrous experience of the fairy penguins' night return to their island burrows, truly a classic event on the eco-tourist calendar. I was also hoping, you know, she'd bring along some cakes.

Astrid jumped at the chance, so we set off on the long drive to Phillip Island. We were quite tired when we arrived, but the chill evening air and a sliver of Tarte Normande aux Pommes perked us up no end. Our little posse made its way across the dunes to stands erected on the beachfront, and Astrid, dressed to the nines, didn't make a single comment as the heels of her pale yellow Raymond Castle shoes sank deep in the damp and ravaged sand. I could tell she was loving every minute. Who wouldn't?

We huddled together on a hard wooden bench and stared at the pitch dark. We listened to howling wind and crashing waves. Just us and 46,000 Japanese tourists. Astrid was still loving it. I could tell.

Occasionally a gull screeched overhead and a murmur of excitement spread through the crowd. Please remain quiet, said the loudspeaker. Remain seated. Do not use a camera. Then it said it all in Japanese. Astrid, clutching an Oroton handbag on her knees, was nodding approval. She loves rules. She was loving it all. I was so glad I'd asked her.

We sat motionless for another half hour, wind speed increasing and sand and salt spray blowing in our faces. At one with nature. It doesn't get much better than that. Astrid was trembling with anticipation. I could feel it.

Nobody moved. Nobody spoke. Pulses quickened. Waves crashed. Sand blew. Minutes passed. Someone moved. Everyone tensed. Nothing happened. Everyone sighed.

I nudged Astrid and grinned. Her face was numb with emotion. It was obvious. She hadn't even noticed her cashmere coat was dangling in the heath grass. I shivered and said I wished I hadn't left the rum babas in the car. Astrid looked at me, shocked I could think of myself at such a momentous time.

It started to rain. Well, a slight storm I suppose. Nothing that would mar our enjoyment. A streak of lightning shot through the night sky and a giant thunderclap shook the ground nearby. I was a little scared. But Astrid wasn't. I don't think she even registered the change in the weather.

Suddenly a flashlight illuminated the shoreline, everyone gasped with excitement and the loudspeaker said, 'Quiet, no cameras' and 'kotchbotchikotchibotchi', something like that.

Forty-six thousand and two people were very quiet. Hardly breathing. The tension was excruciating.

Two minutes later a very small fairy penguin popped out of the mighty ocean, shook itself off, waddled twenty feet up the beach and fell in a hole.

The Captain Cook landing at Botany Bay could not have elicited such enthusiasm. Japanese to the left of me were hugging. Japanese to the right of me were hugging. Cameras were going off like Fourth of July fireworks. No doubt the head of the Phillip Island loudspeaker department received his pink slip the following day.

I looked at Astrid. She was speechless, her face a mask of profound experience. I felt inordinately proud so many foreigners had come to see the spectacle, as if I alone was responsible for the whole thing, a sort of philanthropic marine biologist. The Honourable Professor Maggie Cousteau Groff. I was just getting to the part where I was made Chief of Operations at the Antarctic Research Station when Astrid's rather loud and shrill Queen Victoria voice cut through the night air.

'I must say,' she said, 'this is an awfully long way to come to see a bird get out of the water.'

Astrid was wrong about the penguin, but right about the Napoleon cakes. I checked. Napoleons are sweeping the Americas. Personally I think they owe a lot to the humble mille feuilles, but I daren't mention this to Astrid. I mean, would you? Best to move on, or as Napoleon told me, 'Go forth milady and impart thy culinary art, for tonight you may be busy in the Corsican's boudoir'.

(I hope he wears those boots. I really like those boots.)

Brandy Snaps

These tempting little numbers are no effort at all, and quite at home on both an afternoon tea plate and an after-dinner dessert plate.
You will need:

Thickened cream
1 packet ready-made brandy snap shells
Icing sugar (for serving)

Method: Whip cream until it forms firm peaks. Carefully spoon cream into each end of brandy snap shells — don't try to force it right through.
Presentation: Place brandy snaps on an attractive plate and sprinkle with sifted icing sugar.

Original Sin Cake

Here is my interpretation of Astrid's celebrated divorce cake. As she will not divulge ingredients I have invented my own method, and I have to say Astrid, it's so much better than yours.
You will need:

1 packet chocolate cake mix (plus whatever ingredients the packet specifies. Ignore icing ingredients and instructions)
1 x 375ml bottle good quality caramel topping
Dairy Whip whipped cream
50g rich dark chocolate, grated

Method: Prepare cake mix according to the instructions on the packet and pour into a greased 23cm x 33cm cake tin. Bake at recommended temperature for only 20–25 minutes, taking care not to burn the base as mixture is more spread than usual. The cake is cooked if it springs back when touched in the centre. While still warm make lots of random holes in the cake with a chopstick or straw. Pour the whole jar of caramel topping over cake, and spread evenly with a knife. Refrigerate for two hours until cooled, then spread Dairy Whip over top. Sprinkle generously with freshly grated chocolate.

Presentation: You have to serve this cake from the cooking tin, so I do this in the kitchen. In private. This allows for a modest amount of secret finger licking. It's very rich so don't present large servings.

Carrot Cake

Carrot cake is always a crowd pleaser, and Hoax Cuisine cooks need to know how to make a fancy topping. No, you are not going to use a packet mix. You're going to do some footwork and find a local bakery that makes a good carrot cake, or put your head in the supermarket freezer and take home a top of the range frozen one. Then you're going to personalise it with this superb topping.

You will need

125g cream cheese
¼ cup butter
½ teaspoon vanilla essence
¾ cup icing sugar
1 un-iced carrot cake
Chopped walnuts

Method: Beat cream cheese with butter and vanilla essence. Add sifted icing sugar a little at a time and beat until smooth. Spread mixture over top of cake.

Presentation: Using the tines of a fork, stress the topping to make it look attractive, and sprinkle with chopped walnuts. This topping is also fabulous on chocolate muffins.

Apple Strudel

There's nothing like the smell of apple strudel cooking in the oven to fill a house with old-fashioned warmth. Truly a classic image-maker.

You will need:

2 sheets puff pastry, thawed
½ cup melted butter
1 cup white breadcrumbs
3 large apples, peeled, cored and *thinly* sliced
½ cup caster sugar (yes, use the sugar from your
vanilla bean jar)
1 teaspoon ground cinnamon
¼ teaspoon ground nutmeg
¾ cup sultanas
¼ cup slivered almonds
Icing sugar (for serving)

Method: Join pastry sheets by brushing one edge with water and overlapping the second sheet, pressing edges firmly together to avoid sugar leakage. You now have a large rectangle. Brush pastry with a little melted butter. Scatter breadcrumbs, apple, sugar, cinnamon, nutmeg, sultanas and slivered almonds over pastry, keeping filling away from edges. Drizzle butter over apples, reserving a little to glaze the top. Fold long sides gently over filling and carefully roll strudel up from the narrow end. Seal edges well by pressing firmly, and brush pastry with remaining butter. Place on a greased baking tray and bake at 200°C for about 30 to 35 minutes. (If sugar does leak out and burn the base, don't panic. Allow to cool, then flake burnt bits off with a sharp knife. Finish browning the top under a hot grill if necessary.)
Presentation: Dust liberally with sifted icing sugar, and serve warm with vanilla ice cream.

Funnel Cake

My first experience with this extraordinary cake was at a funnel cake stand in a Florida flea market. I was totally mesmerised by the funnel cake maker for the day, Randy. In my best Australian voice I asked Randy for the recipe, and like anyone else I'd spoken to in the Deep South, he cocked his head, grinned, and said 'Y'all ain't from round here'. Honest, I never got a straight answer to a single question below the Mason Dixon line, but I did get Randy's recipe.

You're going to like funnel cake. It looks like a spirograph drawing in 3D or, if you like, a multi-dimensional pretzel. Either way people are really impressed by this incredibly simple cake.

You will need:

1 cup sifted plain flour
1 teaspoon baking powder
A pinch salt
1 heaped tablespoon caster sugar
200ml milk
1 egg
Vegetable oil for deep-frying
Icing sugar (for serving)

Method: Blend flour, baking powder, salt, caster sugar, milk and egg until smooth. Batter should be smooth and not too thick. If it is too thin, add a little more flour, if it is too thick add a bit more milk. In a saucepan, heat vegetable oil until hot. Now comes the fun part. You will need an ordinary kitchen funnel with an opening about 1 cm wide. Place your finger over the opening and pour ¼ cup of batter into funnel. Hold funnel over centre of hot fat and release finger. With a quick circular motion starting from centre, let batter flow smoothly into the oil, criss-crossing the pan to make an interesting design. I usually write my initials. As soon as the bottom turns golden brown (a matter of seconds), turn the cake with tongs to cook other side. When both sides are done, remove from oil and drain well on paper towels.

Presentation: Sprinkle with sifted icing sugar and consume immediately. I kid you not; this will really impress the troops.

Summer Fruit Gateau

Move over Tiramisu — here comes Maggie's Summer Fruit Gateau! This cake has it all. It's simple to prepare, tastes wonderful, and can be easily enlarged if necessary.

You will need:

1 cup thickened cream
½ tablespoon icing sugar
About 14 European sponge fingers (in biscuit section
of the supermarket)
1 punnet ripe strawberries (washed, hulled, and sliced)

Method: Whip cream with icing sugar until it forms stiff peaks. Line base of a 23.5cm x 13cm loaf tin with half the sponge fingers. Spread a third of the cream over fingers, scatter half the strawberries over cream, and spread another third of the cream over strawberries. Place another row of sponge fingers over cream and top with remaining cream and sliced strawberries. Cover and refrigerate for at least two hours.

Presentation: Serve from the tin, preferably in the kitchen. Use a fish slice to cut down between sponge fingers, and carefully transfer each slice to a plate.

Letterbox Update

When I was a wee girl my daddy would ask me, 'what's the difference between an elephant's bottom and a letterbox?' Speechless with excitement I'd hop around on one foot until Dad delivered the punch line. 'Well Maggie,' he'd announce, shaking his head in mock despair at my ignorance, 'if you don't know, I'm never sending you to post a letter.'

Strange isn't it how things in life come full circle? I mean, who would have thought all those years ago I'd end up with a postman with a face like an elephant's bottom.

Chapter Thirteen

Savoury Pies and Quiches

In our house we have a word for my pastry: bait.

I don't mind admitting I am a frightful pastry maker. I've tried everything, even pretending I am on a cooking show demonstrating the correct procedure to seven million viewers. Nothing works.

Maybe it's not my fault. My father, who was a ship's captain, told me he always shook hands with the pastry chef before leaving port. According to the merchant navy, cold, dry hands make good pastry, and on long ocean voyages a good pastry chef was considered the most important member of the crew. This may explain why I am a pastry failure. I inherited the wrong hands.

Savoury Pie and Quiche Tips

- Once you have discovered your favourite frozen or fresh bakery pie or quiche, take the foil baking tray to the shops and find an attractive pie or quiche dish the same size. It's best to cook frozen pies in the foil tray provided and transfer to your own dish for serving. Don't forget to warm your dish!
- If you burn pastry on a pie edge, lightly grate with a cheese grater to restore.

- Brush frozen pastry with milk to give a golden finish when cooked.
- Personalise bought quiche with a topping of finely grated cheese and chopped parsley.
- If you ever drive between Byron Bay and Brunswick Heads, stop at The Humble Pie Company on the Pacific Highway at Billinudgel. They make the best pies you will ever taste. The curried lentil family pie is to die for.

The Recipes

I see no point in struggling to do something my supermarket freezer and local bakery do better, so I purchase prepared pastry, either in sheets or ready-made crusts. I have also convinced myself the secret to a successful pie or quiche is a superior interior, although my friend's grandmother, Violet Mason, insists pastry quality is paramount.

Violet will be ninety-four next birthday, born, I kid you not, in Middelfart, Denmark, an accident of mirth she has carried with immense pride, taking special care to complete the 'Birthplace' section on all forms in large upper case letters. In addition to this exciting claim to fame Violet also holds a black belt in pastry, so it was only fitting I ask her for a guest recipe to include in my savoury pie and quiche chapter.

Violet Mason's Spinach Quiche

This is a pleasing alternative to traditional quiche, and perfect for picnics or a work lunch. Violet asked me to remind you that spinach is good for you.

You will need:

1 unbaked 23cm savoury piecrust (from your
supermarket freezer)
2 tablespoons butter
250g packet frozen chopped spinach

¼ cup chopped fresh parsley
250g cottage cheese
¼ cup grated parmesan
2 eggs, lightly beaten
½ cup thickened cream
Salt and pepper

Method: Blind bake piecrust as per packet instructions, usually ten minutes at 180°C. Melt butter in a pan and gently cook spinach until thawed. Remove from heat. Add parsley, cottage cheese, parmesan, beaten eggs, and cream. Mix well. Season to taste. Pour into piecrust (yes, it's very full, but will settle to a lovely thick filling when cooked) and bake at 180°C for about 40 minutes, or until the middle is set.

Presentation: I evict my quiche from the foil tray and place it on a large wooden bread board next to a loaf of fresh bread, and slice both at the table. This quiche is best served warm.

Well, Violet certainly came up trumps. Let's hope she is thrilled to see her recipe in print, although there will probably be a few fireworks at the next C.W.A. meeting when Violet discovers I omitted the pastry instructions.

Violet's Story

If I think hard enough about dear old Violet I can almost hear the thwad, thwad, thwad, as her firm hand rhythmically beats ingredients. I see the large bowl, tilted slightly in the crook of an arm, and the arthritic finger as it sweeps the rim for a taste-test before being wiped unceremoniously on a sensible cotton pinafore.

Many a soul has been fooled by this folksy homemade veneer. But not me. I know that behind the flour and hand-knitted cardigan beats the heart of the Supreme Allied Commander of Melbourne shopping. To date I consider Violet's finest retail achievement to be the return of an unwanted seventieth birthday gift; a floral china tea set. You see, Violet is also, and always will be, the undisputed Queen of Victorian take-back.

Over twenty or so years Violet has exchanged the complete tea set, piece by piece, at a major department store. To her credit Violet never used the china, not from any sense of altruism, but because, as she confided to close friend Doris Ainsworth, she wasn't going to drink out of those friggin' pink roses. Dear me no. Her heart was set on pristine white, with a delicate rim of royal blue and gold. Violet knew the precise make and model she wanted.

Teacup number one was exchanged on a cold wet weekend morning, guaranteeing a young inexperienced Saturday-girl, rushed off her feet.

'Excuse me dear,' said Violet, 'but I've got a little problem. I do hope you can help me.'

'I'll try,' said the girl in an exasperated tone, 'although, as you can see, we're busy today.'

'I know,' said Violet, 'but this really won't take a minute.' She extracted the teacup from one of the store's own carrier bags. A nice touch. Violet is very thorough.

'You see dear, my family bought this tea set for me as a gift, and it would upset them terribly if they knew there was a problem, but I'm afraid the pattern on this cup is much lighter than the others and it simply looks all wrong in the cabinet.' Violet became a little breathless and the girl had to fetch a chair, which Violet obligingly sat on.

'So you don't have a receipt?' said the girl in a recriminatory tone.

'Obviously not,' replied Violet, careful not to sound too defensive, 'but you're a smart girl. I'm sure you understand the problem.'

The girl took the cup and disappeared out the back, for every negotiation in every department store throughout the world takes place out the back.

When the girl returned with the cup she leant over Violet and spoke, as the young so often do in the presence of the aged, very loudly, 'We don't have this set in stock right now. Of course, if we did, we would change the cup. Would you like me to order it in?'

'Oh dear,' said Violet, 'oh dear,' and she fanned her face elaborately with the empty carrier bag. 'I don't know what to do, really I don't,' and Violet had to privately reprimand herself, for there was a fleeting moment when she forgot it was a game and experienced a twinge of sincere concern over the fate of a teacup, totally at odds with what she had come to expect from a nurse imprisoned by the Japanese during the Second World War! 'Easy girl,' she warned herself, 'easy.'

Violet affected a small stumble as she rose from the chair, hoping her grin would be mistaken for a smile of embarrassed clumsiness.

'Of course, there is a solution that would make things easier,' said Violet, and noticed the girl glancing at the clock, so spoke more slowly than usual. 'You see that tea set over there, the white one with the blue and gold rim? Well, I use that in my kitchen, and I've broken a cup and need to replace it. I'd be quite happy to take one of those cups in exchange, and then come back later when you've got the pink rose set in stock.'

The salesgirl hurriedly checked the price catalogue, and finding the cost identical, and the minutes ticking into her lunchbreak, exchanged the cup without further ado. About two minutes later customers on the escalator distinctly heard a little old lady humming, 'Life is a cabaret, old chum ...'

Over the next eighteen years, with suitable intermissions, Violet used the above method, with appropriate variations, on an entire generation of Melbourne Saturday-girls. By 1996 only the teapot remained in pink rose splendour, and practically a whole set of white china with blue and gold rim was resplendent in Violet's cabinet.

It was another wet and windy Melbourne day when Violet arrived at the department store with the pink rose teapot in the correct carrier bag. Violet was thrilled to see another 'new' assistant, and made a beeline for her.

'Excuse me, young lady,' she said confidently, 'this teapot was a present, so I don't have a receipt, but it dribbles.'

The salesgirl, as Violet had intended, was momentarily confused. She had probably, surmised Violet, never even used a teapot. The girl made a muffled excuse and disappeared out the back.

A short while later she returned with a suited, bespectacled, older gentleman who wore a badge declaring in bold black letters, 'Manager'. He was tall and thin with greasy grey hair combed, in a vain attempt to conceal baldness, across his head from the top of one ear to the top of the other. He had the biggest nose Violet had ever seen, and I have heard her, when relating this story, refer to him as half man, half nose.

The manager glowered at Violet, then turned to the salesgirl and ordered, 'Just wrap up that white teapot over there, the one with the blue and gold rim. Get on with it, girl.' Then he directed his full attention to Violet.

'Madam!' he exclaimed sharply, and puffed out his chest, put his hands on his hips, arms akimbo, and paced menacingly up and down like Henry V about to address the troops at Agincourt.

After several turns he stopped, furrowed his brows, and peered accusingly over his glasses at Violet before proclaiming very loudly 'I have been manager of the china department in this store for twenty-seven years, and during that time we have *never* stocked or sold the pink rose china you have returned!'

He stood up straight, clasped his thumbs under his jacket lapels and beat out a satisfied drum solo on the front with his fingers, well pleased at belittling a defenceless old lady, and, no doubt, thoroughly enjoying a mental image of Violet sipping tea in the local prison.

Violet was highly amused, and not the least bit flustered by the manager's outburst, though she took great care to look meek and frail until the girl had wrapped and handed her the precious new white teapot. Once it was safely in her carrier bag, Violet smiled sweetly at the girl and thanked her. The smile was quickly replaced with what we call Violet's 'bad smell' look, a cross between a sneer and revulsion, and she directed it firmly at Mr Nose and Trousers, the manager.

'Listen, sonny,' said Violet slowly, relishing his complete shock at her carefully chosen words, 'I have *never* said it was bought here!'

As I said, fireworks at the next CWA meeting! Time, I think, for some more fabulous Hoax Cuisine pie and quiche recipes.

Aussie Steak Pie

This is an easy and delicious way of giving
the local bakery pie that superior interior I
was on about. It's also immensely satisfying
to cook a meal by simply opening and
closing the oven door.
  You will need:

1 ready-made steak pie — either frozen or from the bakery
1 teaspoon Worcestershire Sauce
1 tablespoon dry sherry

Method: Cook or reheat pie as per instructions. Meanwhile mix
together Worcestershire Sauce and dry sherry.
Presentation: Just before serving, make a cut in centre of the pie
and carefully pour in the sauce and sherry mixture. Allow to stand
for a few minutes before cutting.

English Pork Pies

These little pastry-encased gems are sold in many supermarkets
and deli departments. Pork pies are already cooked, and splendid
served cold for an alfresco lunch, a picnic, or with a fabulous green
salad on a warm summer evening. You can buy either individual
pies or family-size pies. They look small but are very rich and
filling so a little goes a long way.
  Always ask a deli assistant when the pies were delivered to the
store, as the fresher they are the better. You will eventually get wise
to their delivery arrangements and know exactly when to purchase
your pork pies. And remember, they *are* your pork pies. You spent
hours making them. Hours.
  Everyone seems to have a favourite condiment to accompany
pork pies. My personal preference is for an imported pork pie with
'homemade' pickled onions, a glass of Guinness, and rain dashing
the windowpanes, but I also enjoy the heady mix of pie, hot

English mustard, a Clare Valley Riesling and a view of Sydney Harbour. English pork pies are quite nice too with my salsa recipe from Chapter Three.

Old Fashioned Chicken Pie

This is good comfort food for a cold winter's night. It's very easy, and involves my favourite ingredient, a cooked chicken. I cook this pie in a square dish because the pastry sheet fits perfectly on top, but mostly because the square dishes were on special at Big W.
    You will need:

1 sheet frozen puff pastry
1 cooked chicken (amount used depends
on the size of your pie dish)
1 x 500g packet frozen mixed vegetables
1 x 420g can condensed cream of chicken soup
1 cup sage and onion stuffing mix
Milk

Method: Thaw pastry. Cut up cooked chicken, discarding skin and bones. Steam vegetables and combine with soup, stuffing mix and chicken. If mixture is too thick, add a little water. Spoon into a deep pie dish, wet rim of dish with water, and place pastry sheet over pie, pressing firmly at the edges. Cut off excess pastry and crimp edges with a fork. Brush pastry with milk and make a slit in the centre. Bake at 220°C for about 30 minutes, or until golden brown.
Presentation: Always serve Old Fashioned Chicken Pie at the table. When you cut into this pie the steam and smell are quite wonderful and, as I once read in a very old cookery book, very good for your complexion. They tried everything to domesticate us, didn't they?

Tortilla and Bean Pie

Yet another gem from down Mexico way, this time using tortillas instead of pastry. Tortilla and Bean Pie is very filling.
You will need:

A round, high-sided pie dish
1 x 420g can Mexican beans
1 x 420g can refried beans
1 x 270g can corn kernels
¼ cup black olives, stoned and sliced
½ green pepper, finely chopped
1 teaspoon ground cumin
1 teaspoon chilli powder
1 packet tortillas (a packet of 6 will be enough)
1½ cups grated cheddar cheese

Method: Combine beans, corn, olives, green pepper, cumin and chilli in a saucepan and heat gently for ten minutes until mixture has thickened. Lightly grease pie dish and place a tortilla in the bottom. Spoon a layer of bean mixture over tortilla and sprinkle with a little cheese. Top with another tortilla and repeat layers, ending with a covering of grated cheese. Bake at 180°C for 30 minutes.
Presentation: Allow to cool a little before cutting. Serve with side dishes of salsa and sour cream and buckets of iced water.

Pumpkin Pie

I'm married to an American and each November we celebrate Thanksgiving. I find it a good practice run for Christmas — in fact it's a lot more fun than Christmas because you only have to worry about the food. Pumpkin pie is a traditional Thanksgiving dish and over the years I've fine-tuned my recipe to mouth-watering perfection. This is how things stand at the time of going to press.

You will need:

1 unbaked 23cm savoury piecrust (from
your supermarket freezer)
1½ cups mashed cooked pumpkin (butternut)
2 eggs
100mls thickened cream
⅓ cup caster sugar
½ teaspoon ground cinnamon
½ teaspoon crushed ginger
A pinch ground nutmeg
1 tablespoon brandy (or 1 teaspoon of brandy essence)

Method: Blind bake piecrust according to the packet instructions.
Blend all other ingredients together and pour into piecrust. Bake
at 180°C for 40–50 minutes, or until middle of pie is set. If crust
starts to burn, cover edge with a strip of foil.
Presentation: This is a festive offering so I like to poke a couple of
holly leaves in the centre for garnish. If holly is in short supply in
your neck of the woods, a small sprig of mint will also do the trick.
Serve warm or cold with a green salad, or as a dessert with oodles
of thick cream.

Letterbox Update

Native wildlife has moved into the milk churn, and my blue plastic
bags keep disappearing from the poinciana tree. We mounted an
'obbo' from an upstairs window and the culprit has been sighted.
He is a satin bowerbird, and somewhere in the near green yonder
is a garden palace with wallpaper made from our telephone bills.
Isn't nature marvellous?

Chapter Fourteen

Sweet Pies and Flans

Been there. Burnt that.

I have a pie story. Last spring I was asked to speak at a ladies' club lunch. During the meal I sat next to a glamorous woman named Regina who charmed me with pioneer tales of cooking on her remote Australian property. Regina and husband Piers had rented an apartment in town for a few days while on their annual pilgrimage to the dentist, a decent hairdresser, and gourmet food shops to stock up on ingredients. Would I like to come back with them and have afternoon tea and taste Regina's infamous rosella pie? Would I ever?

It was a dainty do. Very house and gardens. Lots of sticky-out little fingers, as my friend Audrey would say. We used thick white linen serviettes with laundry marks in the corner, and there was one of those crochet and pearl jobs on the milk jug. The rosella pie was sublime, the tea Fortnum and Mason, the plates Limoges. Pity about old Piers lurking in fifteen different positions, trying to see down the front of my dress.

Regina, in the face of such adversity, showed immeasurable aplomb and made polite conversation while I sat with arms across my chest and twisted my earrings. At a suitable moment I went to the bathroom, and paused outside the door to hear what Regina would say to Piers. I was not disappointed. She clipped Piers round the head with her elbow and announced, 'If it's tits yer after, Piers Hipley, you kin go stare at that old heifer in the barn'.

I guess you can take the girl out of the country, but you can't take the country out of the girl.

Sweet Pies and Flan Tips

After the last chapter I'm fresh out of pie tips, except for this little gem:
*   Preheating the oven when cooking pies is important. It also allows you to burn your fingers when putting food into the oven, as well as when taking it out.

The Recipes

For these recipes you can buy unbaked sweet pastry flan or piecrusts, or fashion your own with pastry sheets — cooked bases are often too small for a family. You will find some 'interiors' in this chapter are a little off the beaten track, as we mustn't forget an important part of Hoax Cuisine is to impress the pants off the opposition with innovation.

Fortunately for you I haven't given the recipe for rosella pie (by the way, these rosellas were little red fruits, not birds!) because I didn't have a spare hand to write it down. Instead, I have a superb peanut butter pie recipe from my friend Georgia, who is, in her husband's own words, the queen of peanut butter thighs (soft, smooth, and easy to spread). I promised not to mention this, but couldn't help myself. That's you sunk, Fergus.

Georgia's Peanut Butter Pie

This is absolutely scrumptious. It's also deliciously simple to make and sets in the fridge. The bowl lickings are manna from heaven. I frequently double quantities and make two.

You will need:

1 medium (approx 23cm) unbaked sweet short pastry crust
125g cream cheese
½ cup smooth peanut butter
½ cup caster sugar
1 tablespoon melted butter
½ teaspoon vanilla essence
½ cup thickened cream, whipped
Chocolate for grating

Method: Bake crust as per packet instruction, usually 12 minutes at 220°C. Allow to cool. Mix together cream cheese, peanut butter, sugar, melted butter and vanilla essence, and beat until smooth. Fold through the whipped cream. Spoon into piecrust. Refrigerate until set.

Presentation: Just before serving, garnish with grated chocolate. I usually put gratings in the middle as by the time the pie is set I don't have enough chocolate left to do the whole top.

Thank you Georgia, it's a great pie recipe. And now we know a little about your, how shall I put it, physical personality, I have to say I think you would have got on very well with my mate Piers. In fact I think I'll send him a copy of this story. That'll give him Georgia on the mind.

Georgia's Story

When the local golf club announced it would have Andalusian stallions performing in the clubhouse, Georgia just had to see it. Well, you would, wouldn't you?

She bought tickets weeks in advance, knowing places would fill quickly, and in a moment of unbridled enthusiasm purchased one extra ticket so her daughter could take her best friend Holly. I know you're impressed. Georgia's very kind.

As expected the clubhouse was packed to the rafters, so it was lucky Georgia's party arrived several hours beforehand to secure ringside seats. Watching two handlers bring four large horses up a staircase is worth twelve dollars of anyone's money. Georgia says she now understands why clubs have busy-patterned carpets.

The Master of Ceremonies got on the microphone and blabbed about how it takes a hundred and fifty years to train stallions to perform the dances they were about to see, and two hundred and forty years to learn to ride them. Apparently these horses were four of only four in the world who could perform the special manoeuvres to be shown today, so everyone had better flippin' appreciate it. Georgia may have exaggerated a bit there, but you get the general idea, I know.

Then Señor Martinez, Master of the Spanish Riding Academy, marched gamely into the ring. He wore tight white breeches, a black fedora, tight white breeches, a black and red Spanish riding jacket, tight white breeches, long black leather boots and tight white breeches. Like the stallions, Señor Martinez of the Spanish Riding Academy had his goods in the shop window.

A hush fell.

Señor Martinez, Master of the Spanish Riding Academy, twirled dramatically in his tight white breeches, flipped the tails of his jacket and cracked the whip.

Thwack!

Two Goliaths of horseflesh pranced into the ring on hoofy hoe. That's horse for tippee toe.

'Ooooh,' said the crowd.

'Aaaah,' said the children.

'Wow!' said Georgia as Señor Martinez, Master of the Spanish Riding Academy, did a pirouette not three feet from her seat.

Then four riders mounted four white steeds and, at Señor Martinez, Master of the Spanish Riding Academy's command, they danced and snorted and kicked and reared their way through Vivaldi's Four Seasons. In our golf club.

Señor Martinez was thrilled. So thrilled he called for his own horse, Conquistador, a bigger whiter Andalusian stallion that had spent two hours at the hairdresser's. Señor Martinez, Master of the Spanish Riding Academy, climbed aboard. He was, as the Master of Ceremonies pointed out, at one with his horse, and Georgia told me that from where she was sitting it's possible they had the same father.

The girls were totally enthralled by the horses and their dancing, and most envious of the lone female rider. They were pretending to be her. Georgia was totally enthralled by Señor Martinez, Master of the Spanish Riding Academy. She was pretending to be his horse.

As the show came to a close the Master of Ceremonies announced that Señor Martinez, Master of the Spanish Riding Academy, would autograph posters of himself and Conquistador for ten bucks apiece. Photographs would be taken for five bucks apiece. Children could line up near the entrance and pat the horses.

There was a short kerfuffle while Georgia pointed out fiscal details to her charges. Then they lined up near the entrance. Georgia was the only grown-up in the queue. The Master of Ceremonies, assuming she was on day release from somewhere, smiled at her in a condescending fashion and said, 'Did you want to pat the horses dear?'

'No,' said Georgia. 'I want to pat Señor Martinez.'

The queue fell silent. The Master of Ceremonies went red as a postbox. He chuckled and made a hunched gesture at Georgia's daughter before saying, 'Your mother's a one, isn't she?'

'She's not my mother,' said Georgia's daughter.

'We've never seen her before,' said her friend.

Custard Pie with Nutmeg

Custard pies are consistent gold medal winners in Hoax Cuisine. Practically every local bakery or cake shop in Australia makes a splendid family custard pie that will pass for 'homemade'. Even some of the frozen custard pies pass muster.

The major problem with custard pies is getting them home from the store with the custard part intact. I don't understand why cake shops are still putting them in paper bags — it's absurd when you think about it. Ever since the 'sudden braking and umbrella falling onto backseat of car and piercing gourmet custard pie' incident I take my own tin to the cake shop. I won't even trust those white boxes.

You will need:

1 family size custard pie
Ground nutmeg

Method and Presentation: Transfer custard pie to your own pie dish, or a large attractive plate if you don't have a dish to fit. If 'your' pie doesn't already have nutmeg on top, sprinkle with ground nutmeg AND BE SEEN DOING IT.

Fresh Lime Pie

This delicious pie recipe was given to me by an elderly lady in America. It's zesty, and so good I always make two.

You will need:

1 medium (approx 23cm) unbaked sweet short pastry crust
1 x 85g packet lime jelly crystals
100ml boiling water
½ x 395g can sweetened condensed milk
¼ cup fresh lime juice (about 1 lime)
½ tablespoon finely grated lime rind
½ x 300g carton sour cream
1–2 lime slices
Freshly whipped cream

Method: Bake piecrust according to the packet instructions, usually 12 minutes at 220°C, and allow to cool. Dissolve jelly crystals in boiling water and allow to cool, but not set. In another bowl mix together condensed milk, lime juice and grated lime rind. Stir in sour cream and cooled lime jelly. Pour into cooled pastry crust, and place in refrigerator to set.

Presentation: Garnish top of pie with a lime slice or two, and serve with freshly whipped cream.

French Fruit Tart with Ripe Berries

Everyone with a busy lifestyle should know where to lay their hands on a French fruit tart at short notice. Here at Hoax Cuisine headquarters we call it possessing 'The Knowledge', and strongly recommend that those of you moving to new areas locate a French fruit tart shop before putting down a house deposit. This is, after all, what real estate agents mean by the term 'location, location, location'.

French fruit tarts are visually splendid. They are generally filled with a liqueur-flavoured custard, topped with fresh fruit, and finished with a fruit glaze.

You will need:

1 punnet ripe berries
(preferably one of those
already used in the tart)
1 ready-made French fruit tart
Icing sugar (for serving)
Thickened cream, whipped

Method: Wash and dry fresh berries, and set aside. Keep tart refrigerated until required, then ensure it is in full view during the first part of the meal.

Presentation: Place a few berries on a dessert plate and sprinkle with sifted icing sugar. This gives the impression you made the tart yourself, and had some berries left over. Finally, arrange a delicate slice of tart and a dollop of cream next to the berries and serve immediately.

Upside Down Apple Pie

This pie has such a professional aura, it looks as if you stopped at
a patisserie on the way home. Ironic that you didn't!
  You will need:

½ teaspoon ground cinnamon
½ cup caster sugar
3 juicy apples, peeled, cored and sliced
¼ cup melted butter
1 sheet frozen puff pastry, thawed
Milk
2 tablespoons icing sugar

Method: Mix cinnamon with caster sugar. Grease a 20cm square
cake tin and sprinkle base with a third of the sugar mixture.
Arrange half the apples over sugar, and pour over half the butter
and scatter another third of the sugar. Top with remaining apples
and butter, and finally the last third of sugar. Cut pastry sheet to
fit snugly inside the cake tin rim and place over apples. Brush with
milk. Bake at 220°C for 30 minutes until pastry is golden brown.
Remove from oven and invert onto a baking tray. Sprinkle with
sifted icing sugar and place under a hot grill for a few minutes until
top is caramelised.
Presentation: Upside down apple pie is delicious served warm
with ice cream. I don't know what it's like cold, as we never have
leftovers.

Simple Strawberry Flan

Utterly delicious. Nothing more to say, except to warn you to hide the strawberries until you make the flan, otherwise stocks will be depleted.

You will need:

1 medium (approx 23cm) unbaked sweet short pastry crust
1 cup thickened cream
1 tablespoon icing sugar
1 punnet ripe strawberries
½ cup strawberry conserve
2 tablespoons water

Method: Bake pastry crust according to the instructions on the packet, and allow to cool. Beat cream and sugar until peaks are formed, spoon into cooled pastry crust and spread to edge. Hull strawberries, cut in half, and arrange close together over cream. Heat strawberry conserve and water in a saucepan and stir until liquid. Remove from heat and, when cool, brush generously over strawberries allowing it to fill the cracks. Chill well.

Presentation: As this flan is one large garnish there is no need for further interference. Enjoy!

Letterbox Update

Today is a red-letter day. I was working in the front garden when Crusty rode up on his bicycle and delivered mail to a new white plastic bag in the poinciana tree. Crusty waved, smiled, and called 'Hi there'. I am overwhelmed with good tidings of great joy towards my fellow man, and feel like Snoopy on a high-kicking day. Close relatives have pointed out that my joyous response is excessive, and this emotional behaviour could be the start of menopause. Yikes!

Chapter Fifteen

Bread

Women need one more piece of manufacturing equipment
in their kitchens like they need a hole in the head.

MAGGIE GROFF — THE REFUND COUNTER AT MYERS

Twenty years ago I told my husband he was never to buy me anything that plugged in for a birthday or Christmas present. He did not listen, and it was therefore a stroke of pure luck I got wind of an impending bread-making machine last December. You see, he believed the advertising hype and thought I'd be thrilled to make bread at home. Yeah, right. When I have a fabulous Vietnamese bakery down the road?

You watch, next Christmas they'll have us mincing our own meat with fancy electric mincers. Giftwrapped and tied with ribbons.

Bread Tips

- Fresh bakery bread is far superior to awful packaged
  doorstep stuff. And that's a good word for it — stuff.
  Apart from anything else, a fresh loaf looks magnificent

146

on the dinner table, or on the side in your kitchen. Definitely an addition to the Hoax Cuisine image, and a must at every family meal.

- Only masochists buy bread with seeds on top. I'm still chiselling seeds from the gap between my sink and the bench. And the cracks in the cork floor.
- Bakeries will also sell half a sliced loaf — useful on occasions.
- To freshen a loaf, heat unwrapped in the oven at 180°C for 10 to 15 minutes.
- If freezing bread, place in two plastic bags, and remove air before sealing.
- Bread should be stored at room temperature (refrigeration dries bread out) and remember, bread wrapped in paper will keep a crisp crust longer.
- Be adventurous. Try different breads, and if you're unsure what to do with it, ask the baker. Different breads enhance different foods — try rye with seafood, ciabatta with salad, or sourdough with soup. Go on. Be brave.
- If the sauce in your casserole, stew or curry is too thin, drop a piece of bread, crust removed, into sauce. Leave for ten minutes, and then stir well. It will thicken as well as if you'd used cornflour.
- If you've accidentally overcooked meat, place it on toast to completely alter the texture. Add a special sauce and no one will notice. Except my husband.
- There is no point in eating beautiful bread if you are going to smother it in something resembling axle grease. Use natural butter. Please.
- If your home is 'open for inspection', warm bread in the oven to give the house a great welcome aroma. Hoax Real Estate.

The Recipes

I'm sure St Honoré, the patron saint of bakers, is sitting at my shoulder as I write this. There can be no other reason I managed to invent so many bread tips. Hopefully he's nodding, especially about the butter. He has asked me to remind you bread is a dish in itself, and effectively replaces a potato, rice or pasta accompaniment.

I admit to being momentarily stumped when deciding whom to ask for a guest recipe that involves bread. None of my friends make bread, and I could hardly ask Mr Ng the baker, as he would (we hope) be hard pressed to come up with a story of his bad behaviour as a woman. Besides, we will not be making bread, since we don't have time for that.

And then it came to me. In a blinding flashing that took me back almost thirty years to our small local bakery in Switzerland, and the irrepressible baker, Madame Schroeder, and her irresistible Mountain Tartine. It's true. Good things come to those who wait.

Madame Schroeder's Mountain Tartine

A day on the ski slopes wasn't complete without a glass of mulled wine and a slice of Mountain Tartine: Madame Schroeder's wonderful pressed French loaf full of deliciously healthy gourmet goodies. It's not classic Hoax Cuisine, but to omit it would be criminal.

You will need:

1 French loaf (baguette)
1 clove garlic, peeled and cut in half
1 tablespoon balsamic vinegar
2 tomatoes, finely chopped
1 red pepper, finely chopped
1 yellow pepper, finely chopped
1 small zucchini, finely chopped
½ red onion, finely chopped

8 black olives, pipped and finely chopped
½ cup fresh basil leaves, finely chopped
1 tablespoon tomato puree
2 teaspoons sugar
2 tablespoons extra virgin olive oil
Salt and pepper

Method: Cut bread lengthways as if preparing a roll. Rub garlic and a little salt into cut sides and sprinkle with a few drops of balsamic vinegar. Mix together chopped ingredients, tomato puree, sugar, olive oil, balsamic vinegar and a generous grinding of black pepper. Fill loaf with mixture, wrap in plastic wrap, place on counter and put a heavy weight on top for at least an hour.
Presentation: Remove plastic wrap and slice as required. Mountain Tartine, as you may have realised, is a perfect lunch to pack for a summer picnic.

This recipe brings back so many wonderful memories of the time we lived in a perfect jigsaw picture that was our home in Switzerland. It also rekindles fond remembrances of the richly characterful folk who inhabited our daily lives, especially the women.

Madame Schroeder's Story

Firstly I should give you some background. Jay and I lived above a ski shop in the centre of a picturesque village in the mountains near Montreux. I worked as a nursing sister on an orthopaedic ward at a hospital in the valley, and my husband worked as a 'pister' high on the Bretaye slopes, a position that involved skiing all the runs with a spade and playing cards in a mountain hut in blizzards. Strategically speaking, we had the Alps covered.

We locals, for the most part, lived an idyllic village existence shovelling snow, admiring Mont Blanc and the Dents-du-Midi, working in the morning and early evening, and skiing through siesta. On the way home we'd buy meat from Madame Lang's *charcuterie* and discover our neighbours' business. Further details and juicy gossip could be obtained from Madame Schroeder at the *boulangerie.* Information was directly proportional to the quantity of bread purchased.

To demonstrate the efficiency of this method of communication I should briefly recount an incident that occurred one evening before Christmas. We had American guests and were mixing martinis when the Vermouth ran out. A small emergency. My husband donned snow boots, a jacket, gloves, goggles, scarves and anything else he could fit into, seized the torch, and tramped half a kilometre up the hillside to a Swiss friend's chalet. He returned two hours later with a jam jar full of Vermouth and the friend. The Swiss love emergencies.

Early next morning I fishtailed down the icy mountain road in our old Mini Minor and pulled into a garage for petrol. Bruno, the attendant, made his way over to fill me up.

'Twenty litres of Vermouth,' said Bruno with a cheeky grin. 'And by the way,' he added, 'ask those American friends of yours if they know Hans. He lives in Los Angeles.'

'Yes, of course,' I replied. 'If it's anything like our village they'll know if he flosses twice a day.'

This last was lost on Bruno who thought flossing was a fancy ski manoeuvre for negotiating moguls, small hillocks which are great fun to ski around at top speed, though as a general rule I like to hit them head on and fall flat on my face.

Back to Madame Schroeder's story. Towards the end of February my husband and I were finishing lunch in our flat over the ski shop when there was an almighty crash outside. We ran downstairs and out to the snow-covered street. A bus full of tourists had skidded on black ice, turned on its side, and smashed into Madame Schroeder's boulangerie.

Doors and windows were flung open the length of the street. Madame Racine called excitedly from her window, Madame Althaus gesticulated wildly at the noise, Madame Barbie shook a fist at the driver from the safety of her front door, and Madame Rivier made dainty attempts to retrieve her large white Pyrenean mountain dog, Charlie, from the side of the bus where he was busily attacking fallen suitcases. 'Sharlie, Sharlie,' she called politely, but Charlie boy was on a roll and disappeared down the road with someone's pyjamas.

Madame Ranaldi from the *confiserie* took control of the injured, ably assisted by Madame Cormier, an ex-nurse. Madame Cartier telephoned the emergency services. Madame Dafoe fetched blankets.

Madame Schroeder, whose building the bus had run into, appeared white-faced at her upstairs window and looked down at the broken vehicle parked in her downstairs baker's shop. Thank God she'd been in her bedroom. A man I couldn't quite see pulled her away and closed the window. One of her window boxes fell onto the bus and we all joyously noted that the geraniums were plastic.

The traffic was banking up on both sides of the street, accompanied by the usual horn honking. It was utter mayhem. The bus driver wandered aimlessly around in circles, raising his hands in the air and shaking his head. Madame Lacombe went inside and put the kettle on. Perhaps there were English on the bus who needed a hot beverage.

The news helicopter from Suisse Romande TV arrived, creating further chaos as it blasted snow over everyone and through open doors and windows. Several holidaying doctors attempted to treat the wounded, but Madame Ranaldi saw them off quick smart. She'd done her St Johns Ambulance course.

'Looks like the mothers have it under control,' said my husband, and he walked off down the hill to help sort out the traffic. I went inside and quickly put on my uniform, knowing the hospital would need extra help. This was the biggest emergency they'd had in years. Probably ever.

There were fortunately no deaths, and everyone kept saying how lucky it was that Madame Schroeder had been in her bedroom when the bus hit her building, otherwise she'd have been killed for sure.

Most of the injuries were fractured arms and legs and an assortment of cuts and bruises. I went down to the hospital in one of the ambulances with the two most serious cases, both head injuries.

On the way we passed Madame Rivier still chasing Charlie, who was now dragging a pair of red track pants in his wake.

I would like you to imagine the opening scenes of those urgent television dramas where ambulance officers smash through heavy plastic swing doors with an injured patient while a nurse shouts, 'Male, 26, gunshot wound to left chest, B.P.110 over 60, pulse rapid.'

It wasn't like that at my hospital. Oh, we smashed through the heavy plastic swing doors into the casualty department. That's obligatory. But then Madame Roissy, mother of four and head nurse of casualty, hurried over to me and asked breathlessly,

'Who was that man in Madame Schroeder's bedroom window?'

As I said, wonderful memories. Of course there was no Mountain Tartine for the time it took to repair Madame Schroeder's boulangerie, and we had to survive on chocolate for a whole month.

Proper Croutons

I expect you've heard the joke — why do croutons come in airtight packaging when they're just stale bread anyway? Ha ha. I have to say bought croutons do little to enhance Hoax Cuisine reputation. There is nothing as tasty or visually appealing as the disorderly array of homemade croutons in soup or Caesar salad. And they are so easy there is no excuse. By all means cheat on the soup, but *never* on the croutons.

You will need:

Day-old bread
3 or 4 cloves garlic, finely chopped
Extra virgin olive oil

Method: Cut bread into rough 2cm cubes, leaving crust on. Soak chopped garlic in a saucer of olive oil for an hour. Preheat oven to 200°C. Brush bread cubes with olive oil and garlic and place on a foil-lined baking sheet. Bake, turning once, until crisp and golden.

Watch carefully, as they quickly burn. You can also brush and bake whole bread slices, and break them up when cooled.

Presentation: Use croutons to garnish soup and salads.

N.B. I always order a dish with croutons at outdoor restaurants because they are useful for propping up table legs.

Bruschetta with Chargrilled Red Peppers

This delicious combination of bread, vegetables and herbs is perfect for lunch or Sunday supper.

You will need:

1 day-old French loaf sliced about 2cm thick
Extra virgin olive oil
1 clove garlic, finely chopped
½ red onion, finely chopped
1 tablespoon tomato paste
2 ripe tomatoes, finely chopped
1 teaspoon sugar
1 tablespoon balsamic vinegar
¼ cup fresh basil leaves, finely chopped
1 jar chargrilled red peppers in oil (you may substitute fire-roasted peppers from the deli)

Method: Brush both sides of bread with olive oil. Place on a baking tray and bake, turning once, at 200°C for 8 to 10 minutes until crisp and golden. Remove from oven and allow to cool while you prepare topping. Heat one to two tablespoons of olive oil in a pan and fry garlic and onion until soft. Add tomato paste, tomatoes, sugar and balsamic vinegar and stir well. Remove from heat and stir through basil and as many sliced chargrilled red peppers as desired.

Presentation: Spoon topping onto prepared bread slices, arrange on a platter and serve immediately.

Aussie Damper

Fresh damper served with soup is heaven. If I have made the soup I buy damper from my bakery. If I have cheated on the soup, I make the damper. Sort of.

You will need:

1 packet damper mix
1¼ cups milk (or however much the packet specifies)

Method: Prepare and bake according to the packet instructions. Don't forget to knead dough with one hand, otherwise the phone will ring.

Presentation: Serve warm with lashings of real butter. And soup. Mustn't forget the soup.

Croissants with Cheese and Fruit Filling

This is not strictly a bread recipe, but what the heck! Purchase either fresh croissants from a bakery, or frozen croissants from the supermarket. If you use frozen ones, follow the packet instructions for thawing and heating, and slice each croissant *before* putting it in the oven as it is easier to do this while they are still frozen. Quantities for the filling will vary depending on personal taste and number of croissants to be filled.

You will need:

Fresh chives, chopped
Cottage cheese
Croissants
Alfalfa sprouts
Cranberry sauce

Method: Mix some chopped chives with cottage cheese. Slice croissant in half. Sprinkle alfalfa sprouts on lower half of croissant, spread on the cottage cheese mixture, and top with a dollop of cranberry sauce and other half of croissant.

Presentation: Place filled croissants on a plate and garnish with a few alfalfa sprouts.

Pizzawich with Basil and Mozzarella

This is yummy yummy yummy in your tummy tummy tummy. It enhances your Hoax Cuisine image without having to cheat anywhere.

You will need:

4 Roma tomatoes, finely chopped
½ red onion, finely chopped
1 clove garlic, finely chopped
2 tablespoons fresh basil, finely chopped (or use scissors,
it's quicker)
1 loaf crusty white bread, thick sliced
Sliced mozzarella cheese
Freshly ground pepper

Method: Mix together tomatoes, onion, garlic and basil. Toast required number of bread slices on both sides, then place toast on a foil-lined biscuit tray. Spoon tomato mixture onto toast, smoothing right to the edges, and top with a slice of mozzarella. Place in a medium oven for a few minutes until cheese has melted.

Presentation: Do not attempt to slice. Top with freshly ground black pepper and serve immediately.

Round-Dogs and Onions

The first time I made these terrific round-dogs everyone was terribly impressed and couldn't understand why someone hadn't thought of it before. Not a soul said, 'Well done, Maggie'. The preparation is simple, and the result just the ticket for those who dislike tasteless hot dog bread rolls.

You will need:

> Good quality hot dogs or frankfurters
> Onion, sliced
> Round rolls (I buy crusty knots)

Method: Make deep vertical slits along one side of each hot dog — about five slits to a dog. Plunge into boiling water and simmer until heated through. As hot dog cooks it will curl into a circle. Meanwhile fry onion. Slice roll in half crossways, taking care not to cut right through. Place round-dog on lower half and fill central hole with fried onions.

Presentation: Serve with everyone's favourite mustards.

Letterbox Update

Now that we have become waving friends I am considering buying Crusty a 'Menopause Aware Postman' T-shirt for Christmas. If he reverts to his former unpleasantness I shall go with my original idea of a year's subscription to a weight-loss programme.

Chapter Sixteen

Soups

Soup has a special place in the human psyche. And in my laundry basket. I don't know what it is about me but all my clothes attract the soup of the day. It's most annoying.

When I'm not wearing soup, just thinking about it, the very word conjures images of crackling fires, snow-stacked windowsills, and the promise of thawing hands round a brimming mug. And let's not forget the fond mamas who grin knowingly at the prospect of replete tummies and only one dirty saucepan in the sink.

Apropos the one saucepan lark, it has taken me a long time to convince my family that soup may be a complete meal. For years they waited expectantly for another course, only to be disappointed. Yes, indoctrination about the three-course meal has a lot to answer for.

Soup Tips

- Always put empty cans straight in the outside rubbish bin.
- Avoid using too much liquid in soup. It weakens the flavour.
- If soup is too salty, peel and slice a potato and boil in the soup for ten minutes, then remove.

- It is good manners to tip a bowl away from you in order to finish soup (I tell you this in case you are invited to Government House for a shindig).

The Recipes

As I write I have a clear image of my friend Marcia's kitchen. Not the one she has now, but the childhood kitchen in her family home in England. There was a big wood-fired Aga cooker in the corner, against which a motley crew of animals snuggled for warmth. I don't think the enormous asbestos lids on the Aga top were ever closed, as two huge stockpots sat in a constant state of simmer on the hot plates. The left-hand pot was for dogs and cats, and the right-hand pot for humans, and the shocking sight of a bubbling pig's head or other distasteful body parts would greet accidental raising of the wrong lid.

The safer, more pleasant right-hand pot contained what Marcia's mother, Meredith, referred to as 'leftover soup'. It was constantly added to on a daily basis, and in all those growing-up years I don't think anyone sampled the original recipe. It didn't matter. The leftover soup was always delicious, and most welcome on a cold winter's afternoon.

I discussed with Marcia the possibility of writing out Meredith's recipe for leftover soup, but we threw it in the too hard basket, and settled instead for Marcia's own version of French onion soup.

Marcia's French Onion Soup

This is probably the most famous of all soup recipes, and in our school cookery teacher's opinion the only reason to visit France. Miss Soupspoon, so named because she was always stirring us up, hated the French with a vengeance, and in turn Marcia and I hated Miss Soupspoon with a vengeance. This is not Miss Soupspoon's recipe. It's Marcia's, and very rich and delicious it is too.

You will need:

> 1/3 cup butter (don't you dare use margarine)
> 4 large brown onions, finely sliced
> 4 cloves garlic, finely chopped
> 1 litre box beef stock (from the supermarket shelf)
> 1 teaspoon Worcestershire Sauce
> Pepper
> A French loaf, sliced and toasted
> Swiss cheese slices

Method: Melt butter in a large pan. Separate onion slices into rings and fry gently in butter. The pan will be very full until the onions have softened down, so stir carefully. When onions are translucent add garlic and fry for two minutes. If you add garlic at the beginning it will stick to the pan and burn. Add stock, Worcestershire sauce and freshly grated black pepper. Don't add salt! Bring to the boil and simmer for 30 minutes.

Presentation. Just before serving place Swiss cheese on toasted slices of French bread, and grill until lightly browned. Ladle soup into bowls and float cheese on toast on the top. If you prefer, make ordinary cheese on toast with square bread and cut into small squares. This is sometimes easier for children to manage.

I made this soup last night and the adults adored it. I paid children ten cents for each piece of cheese on toast they consumed, and twenty cents for eating all the onion rings. Sometimes one has to step outside one's moral code, doesn't one!

Time to tell you Marcia's story, although it could just as easily be called Meredith's story, for the truth is it's about both of them. And somebody else!

Marcia's Story

One of life's finest gifts, when young, is to have friends with parents who travel and work in exotic locations. A window of holiday opportunity opens upon endless days of languorous irresponsibility, security without direct parental authority and the occasional heady romance with handsome waiters named Pedro or Carlos. It's also free.

I was fortunate to have such friends. Marcia's parents, Colin and Meredith Hayward, lived at varying times in the best spots of the Mediterranean. Colin was a surgeon in the British Royal Navy, and over the years was sent to numerous different naval hospitals in Europe. The majority of postings were pleasant and safe, though there were a few curly years of war zones thrown in to ward off complacency.

Colin and Meredith moved house as often as most people go to the dentist, and Meredith was as comfortable playing tennis in picturesque Valletta as she was horseback riding on the Golan Heights or walking along a stony beach in Hampshire.

Colin was tall and fair and handsome with the obligatory naval beard. Meredith was petite and dark with astonishing blue eyes. Whilst Colin was quiet and reserved in company, Meredith was; well Meredith was very definitely Meredith.

During holidays their three children would abandon school and university in London and the Home Counties, and descend upon the foreign household accompanied by friends and lovers, the latter cleverly disguised as friends of friends.

We considered ourselves very grown-up taking planes and showing passports so I shall not, in the interest of credibility about my personal sophistication, recount the more puerile behaviour of the British student on holiday, such as farting the National Anthem whilst eating a kilo of green apples and other talented goings-on.

The inundation of impoverished hormonal extras didn't faze Meredith. She'd prepare more beds, give hugs all round, and disappear to play tennis wearing someone else's shorts. Three hours later she'd return with half the tennis club and prepare a splendid lunch for twenty-eight.

At 4 o'clock Meredith would run a finger inside her waistband and exclaim, 'I must be losing weight!' Colin, glancing over his three-day-old newspaper, would reply 'Those aren't your shorts,' whereupon Meredith, looking most surprised, would ask, 'Why not? Who's for afternoon tea?' Meredith was, quite simply, as delicious as her cooking, and most assuredly master of the three-ring circus we children created.

I have not, in thirty-five years, heard Meredith say an unkind word about anyone except Mrs Thatcher. I have never seen Meredith lose her temper. But she has. Once. And, according to her daughter Marcia, once was more than enough.

This is the story of that 'once' as told to me by Marcia, for I was short of funds that year and spent the holiday chambermaiding in the Savoy Hotel.

During a break in nurse training from St Georges Hospital in London, Marcia hop-skipped over to Gibraltar to visit her family. Or was it Malta? It wasn't Rhodes. That's where we knocked the British newsreader Reginald Bosanquet off his water-skis. Perhaps it was Malta. That will do.

Rupert, Marcia's younger brother, arrived two days late, wearing a cravat to hide love-bites. Carrying his suitcase was the current beautiful girlfriend, Ludmilla, who in turn was accompanied by a small plump dark-haired girl, supplied no doubt by Ludmilla's parents who had read the 'Lock up your daughters' sticker on Rupert's forehead.

Anton, Marcia's elder brother, arrived alone. He was having a secret island fling with Carla, the vice-admiral's youngest daughter. Years later Colin told me that he and Meredith used to pray every day for a transfer before the old man found out about Anton. And we thought nobody knew!

These holidays followed a rigid routine. Mornings were for action: tennis, sailing, sweeping sand out of the villa, preparing vegetables for the evening meal, and running errands for Meredith. Afternoons were for the three Ss: swimming, sunning and siesta, all of which allowed plenty of scope for us to pursue the other S, safe in the knowledge the grown-ups had no idea what we were getting up to. How naive we were.

Mealtimes were always momentous occasions. Meredith could feed the five thousand and frequently did. 'Snack' wasn't in her vocabulary. She would produce roast leg of lamb, or rather five legs of lamb, salad Niçoise and the reddest juiciest watermelon for lunch, fresh gingerbread and her own blend of Lapsang and Earl Grey for tea, canapés and drinks at 6 o'clock, and gazpacho, grilled sirloin and garden peas cooked in lettuce leaves for supper, all of which was washed down with local plonk.

In case anyone was peckish Meredith would place a large piece of Stilton and a bowl of partially frozen grapes on the sideboard. No one was ever late to Meredith's table, and the small plump dark-haired girl, surrounded by delicious food, was in seventh heaven, and well compensated for her chaperone duties.

Dinner conversations were legendary on these holiday sojourns. Basically they involved everyone telling lies about school grades, exam results, classmates, boring weekends at Mungo Harding's house, sporting scores, lack of funds and where they had been that afternoon.

Colin and Meredith took it all in good humour, teased mercilessly, and recounted tales of misspent youth to Marcia and the small plump dark-haired girl, while Rupert made puppydog eyes at Ludmilla, and Anton bolted down food so he could creep out and hang around under Carla's window. Marcia's parents were perfect hosts, creating an atmosphere of total relaxation and allowing the young to be verbally adventurous without censor.

One evening, replete with food and bonhomie, the family and friends sat around the dining table and laughed and joked about future careers. Rupert said he wanted to be a doctor. Marcia, of course, was to be a nurse. Anton wanted to be a carpenter but was already at medical school in Newcastle. Ludmilla, the goddess, said she wanted to be a dentist.

'Pull the top two and fill the bottom one,' quipped Rupert, leering at Ludmilla.

'That's enough of that,' said Colin.

'And what do you want to do?' Meredith hurriedly asked the small plump dark-haired girl.

There was silence as everyone awaited her reply. The small plump dark-haired girl looked first at one face, then another, as though timing her response. Suddenly she sat bolt upright and declared confidently, 'I'm going to be an actress'.

Well!

Marcia collapsed with giggles, already having consigned the girl to a boring desk job. Rupert and Ludmilla laughed so hard that Rupert fell off his chair. Anton snorted and nearly choked. The small plump dark-haired girl went scarlet with embarrassment. Colin was silently horrified. Meredith was more vocal.

She went ballistic: how dare you embarrass our guest, in my house; at my table; all the food; money spent on education; how dare you; get a job tomorrow; ungrateful little bastards; disgusting manners; how dare you; untidy rooms; bad school reports; Mrs Thatcher; and let's not forget those disgusting marks on Rupert's neck! *How dare you!* It was all there, though probably not in that order.

To say the offenders skulked around with their tails between their legs for the rest of the holiday is putting it mildly. Marcia was devastated. She'd never seen her mother angry before, and it had a profound effect. The sun lost its warmth. The sea lost its salt. Even Pedro, the waiter, lost his magic. Marcia sat on her bed long into the night writing letters of regret and love and lust under Mediterranean skies, and generally ripping Ludmilla to shreds. She wrote that she liked the small plump dark-haired girl though. I still have the letter somewhere.

Our suck-up sycophants whitewashed the outside of the villa, replanted flower beds with geraniums, and generally brown-nosed their way back into Meredith's good books. Rupert even had a go at restringing Meredith's tennis racquet, but it was such a failure that everyone clubbed together, united in guilt, to buy her a new one.

For their part Colin and Meredith doted on the small plump dark-haired girl and courageously ignored fawning and other pathetic attempts at repair from their offspring. By the end of the holiday Rupert and Ludmilla had broken up, Anton had been given his marching orders by the vice-admiral, and Marcia had vowed never to laugh at anyone again.

Marcia did not recount this story to me for many years. Why should she? It had no intrinsic value, apart from the lesson in manners and the fine example of the power of isolated maternal fury.

You must delve deeper. You must ask, 'Who laughed last?' I'll tell you.

An extraordinarily talented, small, plump, dark-haired girl, that's who.

Her name?

Dawn French.

Lobster Bisque

Spoonfuls of culture here! This wonderful soup makes a great entrée, especially if cooking for friends when all effort should be put into the first course, as they'll be too sozzled to remember dessert. As a rough guide, one can of soup will feed two people an entrée-size serve.

You will need:

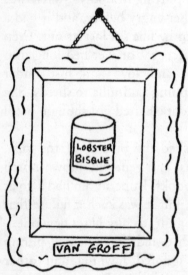

1 can lobster bisque
1 tablespoon dry sherry
Freshly ground black pepper

Method: Open can, pour into saucepan, and discard can in outside bin. Follow instructions on can for heating. Just before you're ready to serve, add dry sherry to soup and allow the flavours to meld for a couple of minutes.

Presentation: Serve with fresh sourdough bread.

Zucchini Soup with Aromatic Spices

This beautiful curried soup is a wonderful way of using up those big bags of home-grown zucchinis that neighbours tend to hand over the fence. It's an extraordinarily delicious transformation of an

unusually ordinary vegetable. Not for nought did the writer John Gould declare he killed the first zucchini he ever saw with a hoe.
You will need:

⅓ cup butter
½ kilo zucchini, sliced
½ brown onion, sliced
1 x 500ml box chicken stock
1½ teaspoons curry powder
A dash Tabasco sauce
Fresh chives

Method: Melt butter in a large pan and fry vegetables for a few minutes on low heat. Add chicken stock, curry powder and a dash of Tabasco sauce, and simmer for ten minutes. Allow to cool and puree in blender. Return to pan and reheat but do not boil.
Presentation: Pour into bowls and sprinkle each one with a spoonful of chopped fresh chives.

Chilled Strawberry Soup

Cold fruity soups are very popular in central Europe and I have always thought it strange, owing to our warm climate, that they have not found a place in Australian hearts. The Hungarians make this soup with red wine, but I find that too strong. Chilled Strawberry Soup makes a perfect light entrée, or a pleasant summer lunch.
You will need:

1 punnet fresh strawberries (about 2 cups)
2 cups strawberry yoghurt
4 tablespoons tropical fruit juice
2 tablespoons honey
Mint leaves for garnish

Method: Wash and hull strawberries, and put in a blender with yoghurt, fruit juice and honey. Blend well.

Presentation: Serve immediately. Remember this is a delicate summer soup, so serve modest amounts in small white bowls, garnished with a sprig of mint.

Seafood Laksa

Asian soups are popular in Australia and there are many packets of ingredients for them on the supermarket shelves. However, for true Hoax Cuisine success it's necessary to go a few steps further than a packet. I use laksa paste and work up from there. Either follow instructions on the paste jar, or use my method and quantities to feed two adults a most impressive and delicious meal.

You will need:

2 tablespoons vegetable oil
250g seafood marinara (buy ready mixed from the fishmonger)
4 tablespoons laksa paste
1 cup boiling water (I find chicken stock makes this too salty)
1 x 400ml can coconut cream
450g Hokkien noodles (these are pre-cooked. Soak in boiling
water for 10–15 minutes to heat and separate)
A handful bean sprouts
4 spring onions, cut into thin strips
¼ red pepper, cut into thin strips
1 chilli, seeded and finely sliced
Fresh coriander

Method: Heat oil in pan. Add seafood and stir-fry for three minutes. Add laksa paste and stir-fry for two minutes. Add boiling water and stir well. Bring to boil, add coconut cream and simmer gently while you drain the noodles and transfer them into large bowls. Ladle soup and seafood over noodles and top with bean sprouts, spring onions, red pepper and chilli. The vegetables should rise clear of the liquid like a volcano.

Presentation: Sprinkle a generous amount of chopped fresh coriander over the volcano and serve immediately.

Grandma Groff's Chicken Corn Soup

This recipe is for a cold winter's night when you dash through the door with a cooked chicken and the doings for salad, and a male family member says 'I fancy soup'. For years I made this meal from scratch, boiling chickens to make stock and cutting kernels from cobs. Not any more. This quick recipe is indistinguishable from the complete works, and just as good. Perhaps I should note here that Grandma Groff grew her own corn and killed her own chickens. Probably embroidered the tablecloth too.

You will need:

½ cooked chicken
1 x 500ml box chicken stock
500ml water (1 litre of stock is too salty)
2 medium potatoes cut into bite-sized cubes
Yellow food colouring powder (or saffron if you prefer)
1 x 420g can corn kernels
Fresh coriander

Method: Discard skin and bones, and shred chicken into bite-sized pieces. Put stock, water, potatoes and a pinch of yellow powder in a saucepan and bring to boil. Cook, covered, until potatoes are tender. Add drained corn kernels, chicken and a generous handful of chopped fresh coriander. Simmer until the chicken is heated through.
Presentation: Ladle into large bowls and garnish with chopped fresh coriander. Occasionally I add a tablespoon of soy sauce for an oriental touch.

Provincial Pumpkin Soup with Ginger Cream

Pumpkin soup is always a firm family favourite. This is an impressive and easy way of adding a touch of *je ne sais quoi* to a humble can.

You will need:

1 can condensed cream of pumpkin soup
1 can milk
Fresh coriander
For the ginger cream:
100ml thickened cream
50ml sour cream
½ teaspoon crushed ginger (yes, from a jar)

Method: Prepare ginger cream at least three hours in advance. Mix thickened cream and sour cream, and stir through crushed ginger. Cover and allow to stand at room temperature for three to four hours. Prepare pumpkin soup according to the can instructions.
Presentation: Pour soup into bowls. Spoon a healthy dollop of ginger cream into the centre of each bowl and garnish with a sprig of fresh coriander.

Letterbox Update

There is a new player in the game. A house in our street has gone up for sale, and the owner, who possesses a bad case of mistaken non-entity, has knocked on our door. Would we mind awfully removing the hideous plastic bag from the beautiful poinciana tree as it lowers the neighbourhood tone? And would we also put the compost bin round the back? And fix the rotten palings in the fence? And if we have any Lladro would we put it in the front window?

We don't have Lladro, so I've purchased two garden gnomes from Kmart.

Chapter Seventeen

Cooking for Children

All for one and free for all.

The visiting children who break bread and wind at my table would give a three-hat chef a run for his money. Just imagine. You serve grilled spring lamb with rocket and radicchio salad, crusty French bread, ripe brie, and a delectable dessert of juicy watermelon and chilled lychees. All is consumed except the radicchio, but heck, it was worth a try.

And now for the interesting part. Each child returns home and informs parents the Groffs fed them a diet of hot dogs, pizza, marshmallows and chocolate sauce. This happens because:

- Children are masters of ulterior motive and hope this attractive menu will put a stop to the oppressive intake of fresh vegetables at home base.
- They cannot be bothered to communicate and say the first thing that comes into their heads.
- I really did serve hot dogs, pizza, marshmallows and chocolate sauce.

This processing of information is known as 'reporting back' and no assistance at all for women wishing to spread news of culinary brilliance. In order to protect your Hoax Cuisine image it is essential you serve the best hot dogs in town, followed by the largest pizza, the yummiest marshmallows and the richest chocolate sauce. Might as well be hung for a sheep and all that jazz.

Tips

- Children should be fed a balanced healthy diet containing lots of fresh fruit and vegetables, blah, blah, blah. Glad that's out of the way.

The Recipes

I apologise for stating the obvious, but to avoid unpleasant mouthing off from condescending food Nazis I should point out that most recipes in this chapter are special treats, and not recommended as a basic diet. Also, on behalf of children and parents in Australia who eat wholesome fresh food each day, I would like to say that we are heartily sick of the term 'healthy treats'. A moronic oxymoron if I ever heard one.

Unfortunately it was not possible for Mary, a delightful gibbon and subject of this chapter's story, to provide me with a personal 'treat' recipe. No matter. In the best tradition of anthropomorphic literature, she has given me a ripper anyway.

Mary's Hot Dog with Corn Relish

In honour of Mary I would like you to pretend this delicious hot dog is a heavily disguised banana.

You will need:

Good quality hot dogs
Cheddar cheese
Bacon, rind removed
Long rolls from the bakery, or a baguette cut
into suitable sections
Corn relish, mustard or tomato sauce

Method: Make a deep slit along the length of each hot dog, taking care not to cut right through. Slice a long piece of cheddar to fit in the hot dog. Wrap bacon round the hot dog in a spiral fashion to contain the cheese, and secure with a couple of toothpicks. Place on a baking tray and bake at 200°C for 15 minutes, or until bacon is crisp.

Presentation: Remove toothpicks (!). Cut each roll, place cooked hot dog in the roll, top with corn relish or your favourite mustard or sauce, and consume immediately.

I expect this is the first publication of a gibbon's recipe. Small restitution for the years of ribald entertainment Mary provided my family when we lived near her home, Taronga Zoo in Sydney.

Taronga Zoo is without doubt the most beautiful zoological garden in the world. Situated on a gentle hillside overlooking the glorious harbour, meandering pathways and convenient sit-upons provide vista after vista of stunning scenery. It's a scented jewel, a constantly evolving paradise of exotica. I've even heard some people actually go there to see animals.

As 'zoo friends' we paid an annual fee for unlimited access to the zoo during opening hours, a sensible move considering we lived a lion's roar from the front gate, and the lions lived a Maggie's roar from ours. Easterly winds transported all manner of animal noise into our suburban garden: trumpeting elephants, screeching macaws and chattering chimps would accompany peg-out time (the one at the washing line and the one face down on the bed), but above them all you could always hear the splendid voice of Mary the gibbon, lead singer in the band.

Operating as a team my infant daughter and I created many games of extracurricular zoological entertainment that involved Mary and her friends, in particular Harold the cuscus. We humans were recklessly naughty, but girl, did we have fun. Suffice it to say, one keeper referred to our escapades as the 'Tales of Two Shitties'.

Time to put on your walking shoes and join me for morning rounds …

Mary's Story

'What she needs is a good root,' said the man staring at Mary.

'Naturally,' I replied, 'your theory is based on the western testosterone philosophy that important female issues, from split ends to the intellectual pabulum posed by the glass ceiling, can be successfully resolved with a bit of healthy rogering.'

'Eh?' he said.

'You believe,' I expanded, 'that one little potent poke from your caveman undies will put all to rights in Mary's world.'

'Eh?' he said.

'Well let me tell you,' I said, 'Mary is perfectly happy *not* ironing shirts. She doesn't *need* someone to start the mower when she's watching her favourite television programme. She doesn't *want* to spend forty years picking up someone else's knickers. She doesn't *have* to buy her own birthday presents.'

'Eh?' he said.

'Oh for goodness sake, shut up,' I barked, 'I don't have time to stand here and listen to misogynist drivel.'

He gave me an odd look, thrust hands in hanky-stuffed pockets, and sauntered off along the path, a broken man, shaking his head at his own ineptitude. I grinned wickedly at my young daughter and she smiled back, well pleased by the downfall of another victim of our secret entrapment.

We stared up into the sticky thick foliage of an enormous Moreton Bay fig tree to where Mary sat proudly on her favourite branch, a position that provided a perfect observation post over her Taronga neighbours, and a splendid view of Sydney harbour.

'Thanks Mary,' I called, and she gazed down with round treacle eyes, almost as familiar to my daughter as my own, except mine aren't treacle, they're more River Thames.

It was a simple game with simple rules. Mary, alone in her enclosure, was given to magnificent displays of full-bodied hooting, a 'noise' best described as the excited call of a baritone owl that could, and did, escalate in pitch to the spine-chilling scream of an injured cheetah.

My partner in crime, aged three, relaxed in her stroller while I settled comfortably on a bench, and together we waited for an unsuspecting human male to stand in front of Mary's enclosure at the moment she started hooting.

We never waited long. Half-an-hour tops. And when the moment came it was like taking candy from a baby, for every man who witnessed Mary's caterwauling would, without fail, chuckle mischievously, look round for an audience, and proudly voice his universal solution to Mary's woes. The poor patsy had no idea Cruella de Vil and her sidekick were waiting in the wings.

In time I learned to screech like a gibbon, which led to another simple game with even simpler rules. After endless practice in the shower, and on the end of Cremorne Point (when that dingbat with the bagpipes wasn't there), I attained perfect gibbon pitch, and could, if I wished, incite Mary to arboreal vandalism by standing under her tree and mimicking her cry. This seemed rather puerile and unkind, even for an expert like me, so I took my talents to the overhead cable car that traverses Taronga Zoo from the top gate to the bottom.

My daughter and I would ride sedately in the gondola until well past the authorities, whereupon I crouched down out of sight and hooted and hollered like Mary as if the devil himself was chasing me. My daughter, a perfect little girl in perfect summer straw, would smile and wave graciously at concerned and horrified tourists on the ground. For some extraordinary reason it always seemed funnier if we were wearing Laura Ashley dresses. I don't know why.

It's time to tell you about Harold. Harold was a cuscus, a harmless Australian marsupial that looked like a large feral cat without ears. As well as disgusting body odour, Harold had a serious claustrophobia problem. In fact he escaped so many times over a three month period I felt the zoo should have erected a sign saying, 'Harold Houdini 11a.m.–11.45a.m.'

Harold's home was a pleasant enclosure in the nocturnal house. Day and night were reversed by means of clever lighting, and visitors could move through a dark corridor, holding on to a handrail, and see normally sleepy inmates prancing around in what they thought was the middle of the night. This didn't impress Harold at all, and by 11a.m. he would climb the branch that was artfully positioned to thwart any attempt at escape, leap easily out of the enclosure on to the handrail, and dink all the way round the building visiting neighbours and depositing scent. I don't think his keepers had any idea of the frequency of Harold's outings for often I saw him do a couple of circuits, peep outside, and hightail it back home, satisfied he had once again bitten his thumb at the establishment.

It wasn't long before the Groffs discovered a fabulous new game that involved Harold. We would lurk in the corridor until our eyes were accustomed to the dark, and wait for visitors to stand outside Harold's enclosure and peer in searching for the elusive cuscus, an action that often took a long time, particularly when Harold wasn't at home.

For ages they would hang on to the handrail and gawp at nothing, while we, in turn, watched them. Sure enough Harold would come poncing along the handrail and stand right next to a visitor and join them in staring intensely into his own enclosure. It took a couple of minutes for Harold's personal pong to register, and when it did all hell let loose. People ran screaming from the building and the Groffs collapsed on the cold hard floor, helpless with laughter. To this day it is still the funniest thing I have ever seen.

Over the years we experienced amazing incidents at Taronga: the Chinese premier's visit, a sedated tiger carried to a van on a stretcher, a donkey eating a schoolteacher's clipboard, giant tortoises mating, and keepers searching for keys in the alligator swamp, but these pale in our memories compared to the wonderful entertainment provided by Harold and Mary.

You may wonder what we did on days when Harold and Mary wouldn't play with us. We were not idle. After trapping our spunk-du-jour at Mary's place we had gardeners to tame for cuttings, keepers to pester for prized bits of fur, shop assistants to tease by squeezing and touching the merchandise, and a creaky old turnstile at the top exit that you could clank through twice in a minute if you ran like the clappers back in the entrance. Bugger the rhinoceros, iguanas and rare tamarinds.

We told frightful fibs to foreigners. Half of Japan thinks the Komodo dragon is plastic. A tour group from Poughkeepsie, New York believes those ghastly swollen bits on elephant's bottoms are piles from sitting on the hot Australian ground. And somewhere in Liverpool, England is a little boy who thinks the red wobbly bit on a turkey's throat pops out when it's done.

So you be careful next time you go to Taronga Zoo.

It's a jungle out there.

P.S. If you require 'closure' on a masculine issue, or wish to vent your feminist spleen against the male population in general, you could do worse than spend a morning with Mary the gibbon. There's no charge for this information. I just threw it in for free. There's nice.

Barbeque Chicken Wings with Honey and Soy

You have two options: marinate wings in a good proprietary sauce, or purchase ready-marinated wings from a butcher or supermarket. The former option is preferable as it allows for what I call 'marinade in action'. In other words, it conveys the impression you whipped up the marinade yourself. Perfect Hoax Cuisine.

You will need:

Chicken wings
1 bottle good quality honey and soy marinade

Method: Pour honey and soy marinade over chicken wings and marinate for a minimum of 30 minutes. Ignore instructions on the bottle that tell you to marinate meat overnight. No woman on Planet Earth knows what she's cooking tomorrow. Barbeque until cooked, basting frequently with extra marinade.

Presentation: Pile wings onto a large platter, stand back and let the troops dig in.

Great Balls of Mire

Of all the disgusting things I have ever cooked, these peanut butter balls are the most deliciously disgustering. Don't blame me if you become addicted.

You will need:

1 cup crunchy peanut butter
1 cup icing sugar
½ x 395g can sweetened condensed milk
1 packet (250g) dark chocolate bits
Chocolate powder (optional)

Method: Mix together peanut butter, sugar, milk and chocolate bits. Using your hands, form mixture into bite-sized balls. Try to suck a mint while you're doing this, otherwise you'll eat all the mixture. Place balls, in a single layer, into an airtight container lined with greaseproof paper. If wished, roll balls in chocolate powder.

Presentation: Store in the fridge until required. Then eat the lot. Great balls of mire are also delicious with chocolate fondue.

Chocolate Fondue with Strawberries and Marshmallows

You won't need a proper fondue pot to prepare this gorgeous treat. It doesn't last long enough to require constant heat. Besides, we don't want little people burning pinkies, do we?

You will need:

150g good quality rich dark chocolate
1/3 cup thickened cream
A dash Grand Marnier or Cognac (optional)
Strawberries and marshmallows

Method: In a saucepan melt chocolate with cream over a low heat, stirring constantly. Remove from heat and add liqueur.
Presentation: Pour into a warmed bowl and serve with strawberries and marshmallows for dipping. And occasionally, great balls of mire.

Sausage Rolls with Homemade Tomato Sauce

Stand back and watch these scrumptious sausage rolls disappear. It's incredibly satisfying to see your hours of preparation well rewarded.

You will need:

1 packet good quality frozen sausage rolls
1 bottle your favourite tomato sauce

Method: Discard packaging and cook sausage rolls according to the packet instructions. Meanwhile, transfer tomato sauce into your own bottle, the one with a label saying 'Homemade Tomato Sauce'. I add a date to the label — adds a touch of authenticity.
Presentation: Arrange sausage rolls on a platter and serve with your own sauce. This is one case when you can fool all the children all the time!

Carnival Pops

I once prepared Carnival Pops the day before prospective buyers came to have a third look at our home. How refreshing, I thought, for them to enjoy these exotic ices on my velvet lawn. What better way, I imagined, for them to learn the endless catering possibilities of my gourmet kitchen? Unfortunately, a junior family member had recently shared my Carnival Pops with Year 2 and re-filled the moulds with pure cordial. If I close my eyes I can relive the joy when, at the salient moment, I inverted a mould and sticky orange cascaded over the kitchen floor. How we laughed ...

You will need:

1 can fruit salad
Ice block moulds

Method: Drain fruit salad, reserving liquid. Three-quarters fill each mould with fruit. Pour reserved liquid over fruit, right to the top. Pop in a stick or handle and freeze.
Presentation: Heck. How many ways are there to present an ice block? Oh yes, I know — present with a serviette!

The Ultimate Milk Shake

I was 18 and sitting in a London Wimpy Bar when I drank my very first milk shake. It was chocolate flavoured (and I use this term loosely), and served in a thick parfait glass so it looked bigger than it was. It was actually bloody awful, but for me, like many impoverished nursing students, it was my sole source of calcium. Certain other dietary requirements were obtained from the four basic food groups of gin, tonic, ice and lemon, and to avoid complete starvation we poor wee girls ordered hospital meals for unconscious patients, and consumed their food at lightning speed in a darkened linen cupboard.

I got caught once. The floor in the linen cupboard on Trundle and Waddington Ward was full of cleaning machinery, so I pushed sheets to one end of a hip-height shelf, put my dinner at the other end, and lay sideways, propped up on one elbow, just like the statue of Lorenzo in the Medici Chapel. And would you believe it, not ten seconds later I was turned to stone.

I had just stuffed a whole potato in my mouth when the door swung open and light flooded my slatted wooden plinth. Sister Miriam was not impressed. I am quick-thinking on such occasions, and to complement my swollen cheeks I crinkled up one side of my nose and crossed my eyes in the fervent hope Sister Miriam wouldn't recognise me.

'Nurse Groff,' she shrieked, 'get down from there at once.'

Timing is everything, isn't it? Two days earlier and she'd have caught me playing Venus of Urbino with Doctor Hargraves.

I'm not sure how I went from milkshakes to Titian, but it was such fun I couldn't stop. I'm back on milkshakes now.

You will need:

1½ cups good quality chocolate ice cream
¾ cup milk (proper milk, not white liquid that has been
interfered with)
4 chocolate cream biscuits

Method: Put chocolate ice cream and milk in a blender and mix until smooth. Break biscuits into blender and blend for about five seconds to spread biscuit pieces through shake.
Presentation: Serve with a spoon!

Letterbox Update

I think I need hormone removement therapy. I had an erotic dream about Crusty the Postman. And him in his Australia Post uniform too. Dear me. They're not making mothers like Theresa any more.

Chapter Eighteen

School Fetes and Cake Stalls

Hell hath no fury like a woman finding a crumpled request note for a cake at 8.30a.m. on the day of the cake stall. In my house, when I find such a note, someone yells 'clear' and everyone scarpers.

The frequency of this occurrence might indicate the purpose of a fete or cake stall is to throw five hundred local households into complete chaos, but it's not. The three main reasons are to raise funds for a cause, to bring people together socially, and to showcase the talents of the organising committee.

Truth to tell there is probably no better forum for advertising your Hoax Cuisine talents, but good intentions often fall by the wayside due to lack of preparation time. Things are different, however, if you are forewarned, but a word of caution. Things don't always work out as you planned, and I speak from experience.

Some memories I can live with but this one still makes me shudder. I had been a clever clogs and branched into Hoax Pharmaceuticals to produce my own shampoo for the school fete. I purchased a bulk container of pink shampoo from a hairdressers' supply company, poured it into small plastic bottles, tied a pink ribbon round the top, and wrote 'Homemade Shampoo' on the labels in pink felt pen. They looked delightful.

It was a real slap in the face to discover not a single bottle was sold. Not surprising either when I tell you someone had whited-out 'Homemade Sham' and replaced it with the single word 'Real'. And if I ever catch the culprit I shall retune his orchestras.

Tips

- Remember that whatever you provide it will cost money, so try not to let it cost time as well. In other words, it's okay to cheat. Right?
- If providing a cake, always prepare the same thing. This saves valuable thinking time.
- In an emergency, which is most of the time, go via a bakery on the way to school and buy a cake. Remove the paper that is on the base, and transfer the cake to your own tin that you thoughtfully lined with greaseproof paper. I always put greaseproof across the top of the tin before putting on the lid — it adds a further touch of authenticity. Don't forget to put your name on the tin so it will be returned.
- Keep all empty jars for jam and preserve making.
- Invest in a calligraphy pen. Might as well impress the committee as much as possible.
- If helping on a stall, wear an apron. It speaks volumes.

The Recipes and Ideas

I'll give you a few recipes and ideas, and from these you can go as far as your talents allow. Be creative, and above all be generous. It's a sad fact but in order to function properly Australian schools depend on fundraising events.

Back in the fifties my mother always came up trumps for the school fete, even though money was scarce. For the most part Mum conformed to expectations but occasionally she produced an outrageous offering. The one that immediately springs to mind was the 'cat' flavoured dog food.

I had been asked by my teacher to bring in a can of something for the Harvest Festival. This proved rather a challenge as cans weren't a big item in our pantry, and the only ones we possessed were boring old dog food. Totally unfazed, Mum removed the proprietary labels on two cans and replaced them with her own 'Homemade Cat-flavoured Dog Food' labels, complete with a nice drawing of a little puddy cat and a large dog licking his lips. I was horrified and desperately embarrassed when I presented them to my teacher, fully expecting a rollicking. I needn't have worried. Mum was the toast of the Harvest Festival!

Most of the time, of course, Mum pickled onions by the ton and cooked acres of sausage rolls, shortbread and apple pies for the school fetes and cake stalls. Those were the days, eh? Thank goodness they've gone.

Mum's Pickled Onions

Don't panic. This isn't the real recipe. It's the one I do!
You will need:

Large jars of store-bought pickled onions
Sticky labels
Some pretty material
Rubber bands

Method: Remove labels from jars by soaking in the laundry sink. Replace with your own labels, noting date the onions were pickled! Next cut out circles of material, preferably with pinking shears, and secure them over the lid with a rubber band. Your pickled onions are now ready for market.

N.B. Remember to prepare a jar for yourself!

Mum's Story

Mum would have been proud of my pickled onion recipe, but cross she didn't think of it herself. She loved to unbalance the status quo and shaking ivy off the school walls was one of her favourite pastimes. I suspect she could have turned the philosophy department at Cambridge University on its ear if she'd chosen, for Mum was capable of drilling any expert into a corner. If she didn't know the subject she simply made it up, delivering her point of view with such conviction that even those who knew she was lying believed her. 'If you are going to be naughty and wrong, Maggie,' she would instruct me, 'be properly naughty and wrong.'

Unfortunately I didn't inherit this unusual skill, though few editors would agree. Occasionally someone with a bossy red pen will mark 'unknown' against a singularly brilliant word on my manuscript because they don't possess, as I do, an 1864 dictionary, but mostly it's because I made up the word. By 2005 I hope to have developed a completely new language. Slang an' all.

My earliest recollection of Mum's talent to confuse emanates from far away days at Castle Street County Primary School. I had returned home in tears, not a rare occurrence for a child who has walked five miles through a snowstorm without shoes, and notified my mother that according to Miss Mavis Rush of Class 2R, Christopher Robin, the owner of Winnie the Pooh, was but a figment of the creator's imagination. I was devastated by this horrendous revelation and sought comfort in the voluminous folds of the living room curtains.

'Rubbish!' exclaimed my mother. She seized the telephone and via our local operator, Mrs Saunders, placed a call to Regents Park Zoo in London. I stopped snivelling and sucked cabbage roses while Mum waited for the keeper of bears.

'Hello Bert,' said Mum, 'How are the bears today?'

Bert said something important and Mum nodded.

'Listen Bert, I've got a question for you,' said Mum, ' Is it true Winnie the Pooh was a real bear at your zoo?'

Mum nodded frantically and gave me a triumphant grin.

'Oh thank you, Bert,' she gushed, 'thank you. I knew it was true.'

Mum put down the telephone and came over and sat next to me in the curtains.

'There you are,' she said kindly, 'you don't imagine a real bear would have a pretend owner, do you?'

'No,' I said, instantly reassured. I knew Mum was right.

'We will tell Miss Rush tomorrow,' said Mum, effectively putting the kibosh on any chance of me having a good night's sleep. I tossed and rossed (red pen here, for sure) until the wee hours, constructing scenes where Mum showed Miss Rush a document, signed by the prime minister, that stated Christopher Robin and Winnie the Pooh were real. I pictured Mum popping next door to use the Claythorpes' typewriter, and Morris Claythorpe signing 'Prime Minister' in a manly hand. I imagined Mum and Mr Claythorpe being led off to prison. I was sitting on the steps of the Peabody Trust poorhouse when I fell asleep.

In the morning it was quite a relief to find the kitchen table devoid of documents, although I was concerned Mum hadn't given the problem her full attention. Oh me of little faith.

After breakfast and a brisk hike down the hillside Mum and I marched hand in hand through the school gates, straight to Miss Rush's classroom door. Mum knocked loudly. 'Come in.' In we went. My knees were knocking. And my teeth. Miss Rush was terrifying. She had a limp.

'Good morning, Mrs Johnson,' said Miss Rush politely.

'I sat next to Christopher Robin Milne at school in Finchley,' announced my mother, 'and he was definitely real, Miss Rush.'

Mum was never one for idle chitchat. Her eyes were wide open and one of her eyebrows was raised questioningly high, daring Miss Rush to respond. Poor Miss Rush went all of a dither and looked around the room, probably for curtains to hide in. I knew just how she felt.

'Oh,' said Miss Rush, 'oh!'

Mum looked down at me and said, 'See Maggie, it's all settled. Miss Rush knows Christopher Robin is a real boy now.' She smiled sweetly at Miss Rush, kissed me, and went home.

Miss Rush was not amused. During first lesson she informed the class of my mother's brush with fame, and of her own incorrect assumption that Christopher Robin was an invention. 'Perhaps Maggie would like to stand up in front of the class and recite a poem about Christopher Robin, especially as her family seem to be such experts. Come along, Maggie. Up the front.'

Even at that tender age I knew Miss Rush was taking a sarcastic dig at my mother, and tempering her own humiliation by embarrassing me. Silly mistake, Miss Rush. Very silly. Hadn't she learned I was the Hampshire answering-back champion?

I'll show her, I thought. I'll tell her the *real* Christopher Robin poems. I walked confidently to the front, took a deep breath, and projected my voice to the back of the room as Mum had taught me:

'Little boy kneels at the foot of the stairs,
Blood on his hands and blood on the mat,
Hush hush, whisper who dares,
Christopher Robin's castrated the cat.'

I was taking another big breath, ready for the next verse, when Miss Rush held up her hand like a policeman and said sharply, 'stop!'

I stopped.

'Did your mother teach you that poem?' she asked sternly.

'Oh yes, Miss Rush,' I answered.

'I thought so,' said Miss Rush.

It was a very proud moment.

Maggie's Chocolate Muffins

I don't mind making a little effort and cooking (?) muffins, as long as I get to the cake stall early and buy them back myself. I buy a dozen chocolate chip muffins from the supermarket and decorate the tops.

Chocolate Topping: Mix a dash of Cointreau into a container of Betty Crocker Chocolate Frosting. Spread frosting over top of the muffins, and for a real touch of class, sprinkle on a few pieces of grated orange peel.

Another alternative is to spread Nutella over the muffins. Don't forget to pack muffins carefully into a large cake tin, and remember to put your name on the tin so it's returned. Empty, you hope.

Homemade Chips

Watch these babies sell! It's a good idea to let it slip that you grew the potatoes yourself. A small note on the label saying 'Home-grown King Edwards' should do it. There's nothing like the royal touch.

You will need:

> A couple of large packets of plain potato chips
> Snap-lock sandwich bags (or any small bags that
> have a perfect seal)
> Sticky labels
> A black felt pen

Method: Oh, you guessed! Transfer chips from the large packets to the sandwich bags. Seal them and write something brilliant on the label — 'Homemade chips' sounds good (actually I write and stick on the labels before I pack the bags). Line a large round basket with a pretty tea towel and pile in the chip packets. Stick two labels back to back, put the price on both sides, and attach it to the basket handle. Make sure your name is on both the tea towel and the basket.

Skullduggery Marmalade

Those of you who were kind enough to buy my previous book will already possess the recipe for Skullduggery Jam, and have probably already worked out how to make the marmalade. For those who haven't, you will need:

> Empty jars
> A large can brand name marmalade

Sticky labels
Pretty fabric with a touch of orange in it
Rubber bands

Method: Wash and dry empty jars. Open the can of marmalade and spoon contents into clean jars. Push down with a spoon to expel air locks. Cut circles of fabric and place them over the lid, securing with a rubber band. Write 'Homemade Marmalade' on the labels, along with the bottling date. If giving as a gift, tie orange ribbon around the top.

N.B. Have I mentioned that I keep bees? Oh yes, oodles of honey in my pots.

Queen Brenda of Banora

Grandma Groff's Wall Washing Solution

This is Groff family folklore and something we often laugh about. When Kitty, my sister-in-law, had her engagement shower in New York Grandma Groff presented her with a large container of homemade wall washing solution, plus the recipe of ingredients. Kitty, who had never cleaned a wall in her life, was more than a little nonplussed and had to be resuscitated by a trip to Neiman Marcus and a two-day hot bath.

Twenty years, three houses, three children and an assortment of dogs and cats later Kitty admits that it was probably the best present anyone gave her. You see, *it actually works!*

You will need:

3³/₄ litres water
¼ cup baking soda
½ cup white vinegar
1 cup ammonia
1 litre plastic bottles
Sticky labels

Method: Mix solution and pour into 1 litre plastic bottles. Using a permanent red felt pen write 'POISON' in large letters on the bottles. Mark your labels 'Homemade Wall Washing Solution' and note instructions. Believe it or not, this sells well at a fete, and it's also a great gift for friends redecorating their houses.

Instructions for use: Wash walls from the bottom up. No rinsing necessary.

Lazy Lamingtons

Children adore lamingtons, and they are big sellers at a school cake stall. This is a wonderful last-minute idea.

You will need:

1 large packet supermarket lamingtons
Lolly bags (like the ones for children's parties)
Rubber bands
Sticky labels

Method: Put one lamington into each lolly bag and secure the top with a rubber band. Write 'Homemade Lamington' on the labels and stick one on each bag. For added panache, pile them into a round basket lined with a pretty tea towel.

Invisible Ink

This is a novel idea and should really impress the fundraising committee. It's for those who don't mind splashing out a few dollars for a bit of fun. The idea is to have attractive glass bottles that people will want to buy for their own spices, except your bottles are full of invisible ink!

You will need:

Little glass bottles
(available from hardware stores, kitchen shops and $2 shops)
Different coloured ribbons
Small sticky labels
A black felt pen

Method: Don't put anything in the bottle! Write 'Invisible Ink' on the labels and stick one neatly on each bottle. Tie ribbons in a neat little bow around the neck. Pile bottles into a basket lined with a pretty tea towel. Stick two labels back to back, note the price, and attach to the basket handle.

Letterbox Update

The plastic bags are again disappearing from the poinciana tree. But never fear. Captain Crusty and his bicycle have admitted defeat and boldly gone where no postman has gone before — to our front door! Yes. Crusty knocked, and when I opened the door he handed me a pile of letters.

Have I won?

Did he rub my letters on his bottom first?

Chapter Nineteen

Christmas

Planning the Christmas menu is like sailing a ship. There can be only one captain.

— MEMO TO ALL STAFF FROM CAPTAIN MAGGIE GROFF

Christmas is a time of great joy, though just who's having the joy is not always clear. It certainly wasn't me when I contracted food poisoning three days before Christmas 1990. I was beyond caring about guests, but managed to rally weakly and tell my husband I had ordered a turkey and he was to collect it from the poultry shop at 6 o'clock on Christmas Eve. I remember falling back onto the pillow thinking I looked all pale and interesting, and saying, 'I've done it all. I've arranged everything. You go and enjoy yourself.'

It never occurred to me that this man who knew everything there was to know about me was unaware each year, in true Hoax Cuisine tradition, I ordered a gourmet stuffed turkey from the poultry shop, which they also cooked, carved, reassembled and wrapped in double foil before I collected it on Christmas Eve. I assumed he knew I reheated it the next day and pretended to have prepared the bird myself. I thought the Christmas Day praise was his way of playing the game.

Apparently not. At 8 o'clock on Christmas Eve he ran into our bedroom and announced in panic, 'There's been a terrible mistake. Someone's given me the wrong turkey. It's all cut and cooked and stuff. I've tried taking it back to the shop but it's shut. Oh God Maggie, I'm so sorry.'

A sudden rush of adrenaline gave me the strength to sit up. My hands slapped my cheeks in horror.

'Oh no,' I wailed, 'How awful. Christmas is completely ruined!'

Christmas Tips

- If someone asks 'Would you like to go away for Christmas?' answer 'Yes,' and start packing.
- Take shortcuts at every available opportunity. It's your Christmas too.
- Purchase a cooked ham from the butcher.
- Purchase special gourmet chutney to accompany the Christmas ham and cold turkey, both in sandwiches and on salad plates. As this is the final chapter you will have figured that you transfer the chutney to your own bottle with your own special Christmas label. Remember two bottles of the same chutney transferred into one large bottle gives greater homemade authenticity. So what if it costs $12. Kudos is priceless.

- Be brave. Buy a panettone — that cake-like thing in the interesting box you've been eyeing at the supermarket. Panettone is a traditional Italian Christmas cake, and delicious thinly sliced and thickly buttered for afternoon tea. Or breakfast. Or whatever. It also made an excellent bread and butter pudding in my pre Hoax Cuisine days.
- Purchase a good quality Christmas pudding. It's far cheaper than making one yourself, a lot less effort, and you won't have five half-full bags of dried fruit rotting in the pantry for the rest of the year.
- Make mince pies. I buy 5 boxes of Mr Kipling's mince pies, which translates to a cake tin full of 30 of the best mince pies you've ever tasted. No one here has figured out I don't make them. Until now.
- Substitute leftover turkey for all recipes calling for cooked chicken in Chapter Three.
- Substitute leftover turkey for the delicious chicken and brie sandwich in Chapter Nine.
- The recipe for my superb Chocolate Christmas Log is on page 17 of my other book, *Mothers Behaving Badly*.

The Recipes

Hands up all those who fell for the Australian 'traditional' seafood on Christmas Day lark? Traditional? Bah, humbug! Christmas is about creating memories, not bad smells in the garbage. Show me a woman preparing seafood and I'll show you a frantic Christmas Eve shopper paying exorbitant prices for seafood and poor quality salad ingredients.

I did it once. I squandered an entire morning of family bonhomie and Barbie accessory construction time preparing interesting bowls of greenery. My fridge looked like Manet's garden. Everyone was hungry again at suppertime, and guess what? No turkey leftovers for sandwiches! Score so far: Turkey 22, Seafood 0.

Apart from roast turkey, another tradition in our family is my mother's Christmas trifle. It was such a treat in cold postwar

England to have a dessert of fruit and jelly and cream and all things pink and chocolate and white. Mum decorated the top with freshly whipped cream from Tom Parker's dairy, and made it look like a snow scene by positioning little fir trees and snowmen between the peaks. I still make it each year and, apart from rekindling fond childhood memories, it's a wonderful accompaniment to cold turkey salad the day after Christmas.

Mum's Christmas Trifle

I've just remembered something. For several years Mum abandoned snow scenes and went artistic ballistic with red and green glace cherries, and bright green stick things called angelica. I used to carefully remove the cherries, cut them in half, eat one side and reposition the other back on the trifle.

You will need:

1 sponge roll
1 large can (825–850g) good quality fruit salad in syrup
1 x 85g packet strawberry jelly crystals
100ml boiling water
1 packet instant pudding mix (chocolate or strawberry, or make a thick setting custard)
600ml cold milk (or however much the instant pudding calls for)
1 x 300ml carton thickened cream
Red and green glace cherries (or snowmen and trees for decoration)
And a partridge in a pear tree (just kidding)

Method: Line base of a glass dessert bowl with slices of sponge roll, and place half-slices around sides. Drain fruit salad and reserve liquid. Spoon fruit over sponge. Dissolve jelly crystals in 100ml boiling water and add reserved syrup to make up a total of 500ml. Mix well, adding extra water if volume is short. Pour liquid over fruit and refrigerate until set — sometimes it settles below sponge and fruit, but this doesn't matter. Prepare instant pudding according to the packet instructions, or make thick custard, and spread over fruit, sponge and jelly. Refrigerate until firm. Whip cream until firm peaks form. Spread cream over trifle, whipping up snow drifts with a fork!

Presentation: Have fun with fir trees and snowmen or dot the top with brightly coloured glacé cherries.

Truly delicious. Just like my mother who, if you haven't guessed, is again the subject of a chapter's story. Come to think of it, I have so many stories about Mum I should probably consider writing a book about her. I shall call it *A Beginner's Guide to Embarrassing your Children* because that was her best subject.

This Christmas tale involves characters that truly enriched my childhood. It also showcases Mum's favourite mathematical brainteaser, a perplexing problem she managed to trot out in various guises over the years. Even after all this time I still cannot fathom the mathematics, and it gives me a warm and fuzzy feeling thinking of you all trying to work it out. It makes a great game for after Christmas lunch — heaps more fun than pinning the ear on Van Gogh — but don't bother sorting it out using real money and condiments for players because that doesn't work. I've tried.

Mum's Christmas Story

The Very Reverend Mr Enderby-Jones was the bane of my mother's life. She believed that Mr Enderby-Jones, God bless his vainglorious soul, awoke every morning, looked from his window, and decided today would be a good day to drive Mrs Johnson up the wall.

My father's job as a master mariner required his presence at sea for great stretches at a time. I think it offended Mr Enderby-Jones' sense of fair play that Mum, left at home to bring up two children, didn't fall apart at the seams like a pathetic wailing damsel in distress. She didn't need Mr Enderby-Jones, saver of souls and shoulder to lean on, and that, I suppose, was the ultimate challenge.

E.J., as we children called him, was vicar of the local parish church and officiated at christenings, marriages and funerals. Dad called him the Vicar of Hatch, Match and Dispatch. Mum called him that sodding old twit in a dress.

E.J. was also the scoutmaster, tennis coach, flower arranger for weddings, secretary of the South Downs Stamp Association, father of the only hairdresser in the high street, star member of the local bowls team, owned the building which housed the bank and taught religious education in our school. It was impossible to pass a day without your path crossing his, and E.J. had a foot in every door in town, except ours.

Reverend Enderby-Jones.

He was a tall thin man with a big pointy nose, a long neck and not much of a chin. Mum used to say that if you stuck black feathers in his dog collar E.J. would make a passable vulture for the school play, but we never asked him because there wasn't much call for vultures in our school plays. It was a very narrow education.

E.J. had the best dress-ups. Long black or white dresses for church with brightly coloured silk draped around the neck, smart khaki shorts and shirts for the scouting outings, snappy white sports numbers for tennis and bowls, and wafty black cloaks for schooldays. I was insanely jealous. Sometimes, when he attended school to spread the good word, I would bang the blackboard duster on the teacher's chair before he arrived, and E.J. would sit down, then spend the rest of the day billowing about the corridors in a beautifully ironed black cloak with a dirty white bottom. It was most satisfying.

E.J. snorted a lot, especially when he was pleased with himself, which was most of the time. For such a conceited vicar his personal habits were disgusting. There was a fair amount of digital investigation of the nasal passages and more than the required amount of rearranging of the orchestras. Not my mother's sort of person at all.

In order to tend his flock, E.J. drove an old Rover Mark something — Mark, Luke and John, Mum called it. No one had taught E.J. about parking and he would stop exactly where he wanted to be, which in our case was right in the middle of the road outside our home. We could hear him putt-putting up the hill and Mum would call out, 'Hit the decks,' and we'd all lie on the floor very still while E.J. stopped his car and marched round the outside of the house knocking on doors and windows.

He was always on an errand of mercy, and if he'd heard the things we said about him he'd have been assured the Johnsons definitely needed saving. He constantly enquired of Mum if there were things that needed fixing, or places she needed taking, a tennis serve needing correction, even perhaps the odd emotional problem Mum might need help solving. He once asked her if she wished to attend a philately meeting, but Mum, who dried all our clothes in a Flatley drier, said no thank you, she already had one.

That got Mum thinking. There was a problem. Our daily, Mrs Bright, had slipped on ice the previous week and broken her ankle, and was laid up in her caravan. We had taken books and dinners and played cards and let Mrs B win, all those caring things you do, but old ma Bright was bored stiff with pain, Agatha Christie and gin rummy. And us. Wouldn't it be nice, thought Mum, if some of the parishioners clubbed together and bought her a small television? Christmas was coming and all that jazz.

E.J. thought it a sterling idea. Mum found a television for thirty pounds, which was quite a lot of money in those days, and E.J.

asked a few of the wealthy neighbourhood dignitaries, for whom Mrs B also cleaned house, and came up with three kind souls willing to donate ten pounds each.

E.J. putt-putted up our hill and gave Mum the thirty pounds and we set off to purchase the television set. Mum in her brief businesslike way explained whom the television was for, and the shopkeeper announced that Mrs Bright cleaned his house too and he would be more than happy to give Mum five pounds off the price. So Mum paid twenty-five pounds and the television was delivered and set up in Mrs B's caravan. She was thrilled and went all teary and goodness me for quite half-an-hour.

On Sunday Mum went to the church to give E.J. the five remaining pounds, and explained how the shop owner had been so kind. Mum suggested it would be fitting to divide the leftover five pounds, and return it to the people who had donated it. 'Quite right,' said Mr Enderby-Jones, 'I'll do it this afternoon.'

The following week Mum went to visit Mrs Bright, who was having the best time doing nothing except watch television and eat casseroles and apple pie. She thanked Mum profusely and then said how kind the vicar had been giving her the two pounds left over. She had used some of it to purchase a television licence.

'Two pounds?' asked Mum. 'There were five left over.'

'Yes, I know,' said Mrs Bright. 'The vicar gave a pound back to each of the three kind people who donated ten pounds each.'

'Oh,' said Mum. 'That's all right then.'

That night Mum was very quiet, lost in thought. She kept writing things on bits of paper and then looking into space and saying 'hmm'. Then she'd grin a very wicked grin and break into laughter.

Next Sunday we all tootled off to see the vicar again.

'Hello Vicar,' said Mum, 'It was kind of you to give that two pounds to Mrs Bright.'

E.J. puffed out his skinny chest and snorted with satisfaction.

'I was just wondering though,' said Mum, 'that if you gave one pound back to each of the people who gave ten pounds, then my sums tell me they each gave nine pounds. Is that right, Vicar? You're so good at maths.'

'That's right, Mrs Johnson,' he answered smugly.

'But aren't, and do correct me if I'm wrong, Vicar, aren't three nines twenty-seven?'

'They are indeed, Mrs Johnson,' he said.

'Well then, Vicar,' said Mum, 'Thirty pounds minus twenty-seven pounds is three pounds, Vicar. You gave Mrs Bright two pounds, Vicar. What did you do with the other pound?'

We didn't see much of the Very Reverend Enderby-Jones after that. Like me, he's probably still trying to figure it out!

Christmas Pizza

As the turkey says, 'Gobble, gobble, gobble'. Be flexible with topping quantities, as much will depend on the amount of leftover turkey.

You will need:

Thick pizza bases
1 jar basil pesto
Shredded pizza cheese (allow about 1 cup per pizza)
Cooked turkey, sliced
Red onion, finely sliced
Roma tomato, chopped
Kalamata olives (remove pips by pressing olives with
base of a mug — the one you drink out of, not the one
sitting next to you).

Method: Place pizza base on a greased pizza pan and prick all over with a fork. Spread three to four tablespoons of basil pesto on base. Sprinkle half the cheese over base, then turkey, onion and tomato. Scatter remaining cheese over pizza and top with halved olives. Bake at 200°C for about 20 minutes, or until crust is cooked. If base remains doughy, slide pizza from pan directly onto oven shelf for the last few minutes of cooking.

Presentation: Place pizza on a wooden chopping board and slice with a pizza wheel.

Last Mango in Paris Christmas Pie

This incredible Hoax Cuisine Christmas Pie will have you dancing round the kitchen. Mangoes are in season at Christmas so I usually tell people I use fresh fruit for this recipe. Of course I don't. I buy a can of mango pulp, because I'm far too busy to be peeling and mashing mangoes.

You will need:

1 medium (approx. 23cm) unbaked sweet short pastry crust
1 x 85g packet orange jelly crystals
100ml boiling water
1 x 170g can mango pulp
125g cream cheese
½ cup sour cream
½ cup caster sugar

Method: Bake piecrust according to the packet instructions, and set aside to cool. Dissolve jelly crystals in boiling water and allow to cool, but not set. Add remaining ingredients to cooled jelly and beat well using a blender. Pour into cooled piecrust and refrigerate until set. If you have excess filling (bought crusts vary slightly in size), eat it!

Presentation: There won't be time to visit the botanical gardens for real holly, so pop a sprig of pretend holly in the centre of your pie. Cut delicate slices and serve on an attractive dessert plate with a couple of ripe strawberries, a scoop of mango sorbet (Chapter Eleven), and a dollop of delicious King Island Cream.

Reuben Sandwiches

'Reubens' are usually made with corned beef and sauerkraut. I dislike corned beef but adore sauerkraut so a few years ago I substituted cold turkey meat and, hey presto, started a new tradition.

You will need:

Sliced rye bread
Wholegrain mustard (or your favourite mustard)
Sauerkraut (drained)
Leftover turkey
Good quality mayonnaise (or your favourite creamy dressing)
Swiss cheese slices

Method: Toast two rye slices for each sandwich. On one toasted slice spread filling layers as follows: mustard, sauerkraut, turkey, mayonnaise, cheese and finally more mustard. Top with second toasted rye slice and wrap whole sandwich in aluminium foil. Place on a baking tray and cook at 180°C for about 10 minutes.
Presentation: Serve with ice-cold beer. I often pretend to be Hungarian while eating 'Reubens'. I don't know why. Just mad, I guess.

Southern Summer Christmas Cake

This is a scrumptious summer gateau that stores in the fridge. Be creative and, as with the trifle, make the top look like a Christmas snow scene.
You will need:

1 large packet vanilla cake mix (and whatever other ingredients
the packet specifies)
250g cream cheese
2 cups milk
1 x 85g packet instant vanilla pudding mix
1 x 440g can crushed pineapple
1 x 300ml carton thickened cream
Christmas decorations for the top

Method: Prepare cake according to the packet instructions. Pour into a 23cm x 33cm cake tin and bake at recommended temperature for only 20–25 minutes, or until sponge springs back when pressed in the centre (remember cake is more spread out than usual). Soften cream cheese and, using a mixer, blend cheese with milk and pudding mix until smooth. Spread mixture over cooled cake. Drain pineapple and, using your fingers, scatter pineapple over pudding mixture. Whip thickened cream until it forms stiff peaks and spread over pineapple.

Presentation: Roughen the cream with a fork to resemble snow, and position Christmas ornaments in the drifts. If I make this at other times of the year I top it with grated chocolate. This cake must be refrigerated.

Kitsch and Dips

I adore this tacky Christmas tree display of raw vegetables and dip. It's so deliciously 70s, great fun for children to prepare, and a good icebreaker at a work Christmas 'do'. It tastes good too.

You will need:

A large tray covered with foil
Broccoli
Celery
Red pepper
Cherry tomatoes
2 tubs of your favourite dip, transferred to your own bowls,
naturally

Method: Cut broccoli into bite-sized florets and arrange on foil tray in the shape of a Christmas tree. Make a tree trunk from celery strips. Cut red pepper in half and slice crossways. Festoon pepper strips across broccoli to resemble tinsel. Dot cherry tomatoes around tree to imitate baubles.

Presentation: I usually place a Christmas decoration on top of the tree, preferably a star, and some wag always attempts to eat it. Serve your Christmas tree with bowls of delicious 'homemade' dip.

Turkey Caesar Salad with Baby Spinach

Yet another use for leftover turkey, and a jolly good reason not to waste this wonderful meat on the dreaded turkey soup fiasco. The rustic elegance of this dish is superb. Not only is it visually stunning but the combination of crisp greens, salty bacon, juicy turkey, and fresh parmesan makes this perfect for a summer holiday lunch, and certainly worthy of entertaining old Julius himself. Occasionally I quote some of his speeches during the meal — it's always good to let your guests know your talents are not confined to domestic expertise.

This recipe may be expanded or reduced as required, so you can be creative with quantities.

You will need:

2 different types of lettuce (I use mignonette and cos)
1 bag baby spinach leaves
Leftover turkey (bones removed)
Shortcut bacon, diced and grilled until crisp
A healthy chunk of parmesan cheese, shaved (if you don't have a shaver, use a steak knife or potato peeler)
1 bottle good quality creamy Caesar salad dressing
Proper croutons (recipe on p. 152)

Method: Wash and drain lettuce and arrange leaves on a large platter. If you are feeding the Roman Forum you can also use a large tray. Spread baby spinach leaves over lettuce. Tear turkey into manageable pieces, drain bacon and scatter both over spinach leaves. Top with shaved parmesan. Shake dressing well and drizzle very generously over whole salad. Do not toss.
Presentation: Just before serving scatter croutons over salad, but do not toss.
Enjoy!

Letterbox Update

What can I say? Everything comes to an end. The year is at an end. This book is at an end. And, as I write, there is frenzied activity at the end of our driveway. A new letterbox is being constructed from bricks, mortar, Anglo-Saxon expletives and a case of premium bitter. It promises to be a grand architectural affair; something in which a postman would be proud to post letters.

I'm pleased Crusty and I resolved postal issues before it was built. Testament, I suppose, to our mutual respect and maturity. Why, just this morning he rode up on his bike and handed me a pile of letters, neatly secured with a rubber band. I noticed him glance at the new letterbox and smile. Crusty was itching to post something in it. I could tell.

As he rode off up the road I called out merrily, 'Happy New Year Crusty.'

'Happy Manure to you too Mrs Groff,' he yelled back.

THE END

Index